CHALDEAN ASTROI

HOW TO CAST AND READ THE HOROSCOPE

AND CALCULATE STAR COURSES.

By GEORGE WILDE.

Author of " A Primer of Astrology," " The Key to Your Horoscope," " The Key to Your Star Courses and Success," " Elemente der Astrologie wie die Gestirne Leib, Seele und Schicksal Beeinflussen."

———

———

6, CENTRAL STREET, HALIFAX, YORKSHIRE.

SECOND EDITION.

Copyright.

1909.

Kessinger Publishing's
Rare Mystical Reprints

THOUSANDS OF SCARCE BOOKS
ON THESE AND OTHER SUBJECTS:

Freemasonry * Akashic * Alchemy * Alternative Health * Ancient Civilizations * Anthroposophy * Astrology * Astronomy * Aura * Bible Study * Cabalah * Cartomancy * Chakras * Clairvoyance * Comparative Religions * Divination * Druids * Eastern Thought * Egyptology * Esoterism * Essenes * Etheric * ESP * Gnosticism * Great White Brotherhood * Hermetics * Kabalah * Karma * Knights Templar * Kundalini * Magic * Meditation * Mediumship * Mesmerism * Metaphysics * Mithraism * Mystery Schools * Mysticism * Mythology * Numerology * Occultism * Palmistry * Pantheism * Parapsychology * Philosophy * Prosperity * Psychokinesis * Psychology * Pyramids * Qabalah * Reincarnation * Rosicrucian * Sacred Geometry * Secret Rituals * Secret Societies * Spiritism * Symbolism * Tarot * Telepathy * Theosophy * Transcendentalism * Upanishads * Vedanta * Wisdom * Yoga * Plus Much More!

DOWNLOAD A FREE CATALOG
AND
SEARCH OUR TITLES AT:

www.kessinger.net

CONTENTS.

Chapter	Pages
Index	4
Preface	5-6
I.—Introduction	7-13
II.—Symbols, Abbreviations, and Glossary	14-20
III.—Explanation of the Twelve Houses of Heaven and their Astrological Signification	21-23
IV.—Probable Description of Persons produced by each of the Signs when ascending and no Planet therein	24-26
V.—Probable Description of Person produced by the different Planets ascending in each of the Signs	27-40
VI.—The Natural Quality, Influences and Effects of the Planets	41-48
VI. & VII.—The Planets in the Houses	47-55
VIII.—The Effects of the Conjunction of Significators—The Effects of the Sextiles, Semi-sextiles, Semi-quintiles, Quintiles, Septiles, Biquintiles, and Trines of Significators—The Effects of Squares, Semi-squares, Sesquiquadrates, and Oppositions of Significators	56-66
IX.—How to Cast the Horoscope	67-69
X.—How to Place the Planets in the Horoscope	70-71
XI.—Health	72-78
XII.—Mental Qualities and Disposition	79-80
XIII.—Pecuniary Prospects	81-84
XIV.—The Employment	85-87
XV.—Marriage: Offspring: Twins	88-91
XVI.—Travelling	92-93
XVII.—Friends and Enemies	94-95
XVIII.—Star Courses	96-109
XIX.—Example: Mr. Pearson's Horoscope	110-120
XX.—Star Course Experiences and Mr. L.'s Horoscope	121-125
XXI.—How to Compute a Horoscope for South Latitude	126-127
XXII.—Star Courses: Examples and Lessons	142-143-146-150
XXII.—Instructions in the Calculations of Star Courses	138-142
XXII.—Transits of Promittors	144-145

INDEX.

	PAGES
Aspects	17
Aspects, Mundane	19
Astrology, Origin of	8
Dragon's Head and Cauda	14-45-46
Diseases attributed to the Planets and Signs of the Zodiac	72-78
Ephemeris and Tables of Houses	67-68-131-134
Standard Time and Greenwich Meantime	128-130
Jupiter in the Ascendant	29-30
Moon in the Ascendant	38-39
Mercury in the Ascendant	36-37
Mars in the Ascendant	30-32
Neptune, Influence of	46-48
Neptune in the Ascendant	46
Orbs: Applying and Separating	20
Planets, Symbols of	14
Planets in the Ascendant	27-46
Planets, Orbs of	16-18-19-20
Promittors Defined	20-96-109
Saturn in the Ascendant	28-29
Significators Defined	56
Stars in their Courses	96-109
Sun in the Ascendant	32-34
Test Horoscope	110-120
Transits	144-145
Uranus in the Ascendant	39-40
Uranus, Influence of	39-41
Venus in the Ascendant	34-35

PREFACE.

A MANUAL of astrology may be roughly described as intended for the service of three classes of persons—astrologers, students of astrology, and inquirers.

The manual now published may be confidently recommended as fully adapted to the needs of the two former classes of individuals. It contains everything that can reasonably be expected to be found in such a work. The exposition is simple and intelligent. The author possesses as much experience, as much ability, and what is equally important, as much candour and love of truth, as will easily be found in any contemporary astrologer.

If, nevertheless, the work should appear to contain some things which a critical judgment might have deemed better omitted, it must be remembered that the task of preparing a manual for students is not an altogether easy one. While nothing demonstrably incorrect must be stated on the authority of general belief or ancient tradition, many dubious matters are not yet disproved, and an introduction to the science which failed to notice them would be confessedly imperfect.

Great caution, nevertheless, is necessary to avoid putting stumbling-blocks into the way of the inquirer, who may easily be provoked to abandon the study if he finds reason to doubt the truth of what he has been confidently told. He ought to understand from the first that, like other sciences, astrology has its certainties, but also its mere probabilities; its truths, but also its errors.

The criterion between them is fortunately a very simple one. It may be asserted with confidence that whatever is really essential to astrology is, to a candid mind, susceptible of demonstration. The influences attributed to the planets, the qualities of their aspects among themselves, the effects of their various positions in the horoscope, the chief rules by which astrologers have in all ages judged concerning body, mind, and fortune, can be shown to be agreeable to experience, and verifiable by such a mass of testimony as equal to that producible in support of any other science. The uncertainties mainly relate either to calculations of the times of events, which must of necessity be difficult and obscure; or to opinions on points of minor importance which might all be invalidated without in any way impairing the evidence for astrology.

It must be admitted that the overwhelming mass of testimony which we have stated to exist will not be found in this manual, or in any other, simply because it is far too extensive. The great use of such books, in so far as concerns the student, is to set him to inquire for himself. Let him go abroad and hunt for evidence. He will soon be delighted by the con'ormity between what he discovers and what he has been taught, in so far as concerns essentials. He will have the pleasure of reflecting that what he finds must be reliable, because he finds it for himself and does not derive it from a book prepared to be set before him. But let him not be discouraged if he finds reason for scepticism as regards many insignificant matters, and let him accept no statement whatever until he has verified it several times.

Nothing—unless it be the ill-advised attempt to predict the future with mathematical accuracy, and its connection in the popular mind with the species of fortune-telling called horary astrology—has brought scientific astrology into such disrepute as the notion that it is "an occult science." It is nothing of the kind. An occult science is one that can be pursued only by adepts. Astrology is just as much a physical science as astronomy or geology. It depends, like them, upon the evidence of ascertained facts, and has so far the advantage of its sister sciences that these facts are patent to the observation of everybody, and that its rules and methods can be mastered by any person of average intelligence. It could not be more grossly misrepresented than by being connected in any way with magic or theosophy. Unfortunately the interest recently excited in these subjects has of late led several astrologers to associate it with them, hoping, probably, thus to obtain more attention for it. They have obtained attention, indeed, but by no means of a flattering nature. It is not intended to denounce or discourage the pursuit of occult studies, but simply to insist that they have nothing to do with astrology, which is a physical and verifiable science or it is nothing. The student, if he is to achieve any useful end, must study it precisely as he would study astronomy; regarding it, in fact, as astronomy brought down from heaven to earth, and employed for the investigation of human life.

A. G. TRENT.

CHAPTER I.

INTRODUCTION.

In the dark ages astrology was thought to be one of the subjects associated with black magic: indeed, the writer is personally acquainted with a rather clever man, a barrister, who once edited the reprint of an old book on astrology, and was in consequence, cut off without the proverbial shilling by an irate bachelor uncle, who denounced his nephew for editing a book on what he called the blackest of black magic.

Astrology has really nothing in common with magic of any kind, white or black. Magic was largely practised in Egypt: whereas astrology had its birth, not in Egypt as Sir Isaac Newton thought, but in Chaldea, and its students were simple shepherds; afterwards called Wise Men. They read the destinies of men from the Conjunctions, and aspects of the planets in the Celestial signs of the Zodiac. These genethliacal themes the Greeks subsequently called horoscopes. These simple folks saw nothing greater, nothing more beautiful than these glorious orbs of a far-off heaven. They regarded with awe and reverence old Sol, as he shot up into the sky at early morn, throwing out his inspiring rays as he soared aloft and then sank to rest in the eventide. We can hardly refuse to forgive them for their simple worship of so smiling and majestic a luminary. The fair "Cynthia," as she lit up their serene skies, impressed them perhaps more than the more distant but not less brilliant Venus. They were evidently keenly intuitive, these guardians of flocks, for they observed the gloominess of the child born when Saturn was in the ascendant. They were obviously struck with the vivacity and gaiety of temperament when Venus succeeded that planet. They observed the buoyant and optimistic temperament, the genial child, when Jupiter held sway.

They detected the baleful influence to the child when the Sun was opposed to or in conjunction with Saturn. They found that the same aspects to Mars produced a brave, warlike, reckless, adventurous child; and so this heavenly wisdom grew. The child born to-day is a living witness of the truth of these old Chaldeans' observations. The child of Mars has all the volcanic qualities as of yore; even though he may try to hide them. The children of Saturn are just as reticent and as sad, whilst

Jupiter's child has lost none of his genial optimism. The child of Venus is still merry and fun-loving.

Astrology has withstood edicts, assaults by those who could not cast a horoscope correctly to save their lives, and attacks by flimsy writers in the Press whose ignorance of the subject makes one blush for them.

It was in Greece that astrology became associated with philosophy; starting from there in the first flight of sciences through the Greek and Roman world it became associated with medicine and religion. The Egyptians had already disfigured the old Chaldean traditions by associating the subject with magic.

There has been endless controversy as to whether astrology originated in Egypt or Chaldea, but Mr. Hogarth's research (see *Authority and Archæology*, page 134) proves that Petosiris, who was thought to be an Egyptian Astrologer, was really a Chaldean; the name was really imported into Egypt. The language of Tema was Aramaean, nearly akin to Chaldean. The oldest known works on astrology are the tablets of Sargon I. of Agadi, who lived 3,800 years before Christ.

Astrology, therefore, is the oldest of all the sciences; it has its votaries in every land; they are to be found in China, India, in Europe, and certainly great progress seems to have been made in recent years in the study of this subject, judging from the rapid increase of aphorisms and the publication of books solely devoted to astrology.

The astrologer contends that man may evade the adverse stellar influences, and that he may avail himself of the propitious influences. To take a concrete example—suppose a person has the luminaries and Saturn in unfriendly aspect, the Astrologer, from calculations, will readily ascertain the periods when financial disaster is threatened, and will give the forewarning which will avert the disaster. There is nothing occult about this science of the stars, there is no invocation, the influence is real, though it is as hard to explain and as inexplicable as gravitation.

Curiously enough, people who do not believe the least bit in astrology, quite unconsciously record their experiences which could only be explained astrologically. Take the case of John Stuart Mill; we all know that he records in his biography how in the autumn of 1826 he fell into a strange and to him unaccountable melancholy, which continued into the next year. On looking at his horoscope we found that Saturn was transiting his Moon's place, which is the notorious planet for producing melancholy. We have all heard of the Saturnine nature; but the Chaldeans had observed this gloominess 5,800 years ago. The old Chaldeans always associated the cross aspects of Mars with accidents. Now witness the fact, that the manuscript of Carlyle's *French Revolution* was accidently burnt when Mars was transiting the Moon's place nine years later. Another gentleman was thrown when hunting under adverse transits. It is, of course, quite impossible to indicate the exact nature of an event, though the writer predicted a titular honour for a person from an aspect of Jupiter, and he found himself, much to his astonishment, in the King's Birthday Honours list.

Many years ago we published a chapter in *Natal Astrology* and said that the laws of planetary influence harmonise with those of heredity. If a mental trait or physical characteristic is strongly marked in both parent and child, that trait or characteristic will be clearly shown in both horoscopes. On the other hand, if parent and child are found to have little or nothing in common, their horoscopes will also be found to be dissimilar. In such cases the child has inherited its peculiarities or distinctive marks of character from the grandparents or the great-grandparents.

A gentleman of our acquaintance has certain positions in his horoscope which produce certain qualities. His only daughter also possesses these characteristics, and they are portrayed in her horoscope though considerably modified by traits of character received from the mother. The daughter's eldest boy is an exact reproduction of his grandfather as his horoscope plainly declares. The grandmother had organic weakness of the heart, though this weakness was more perceptible in the daughter. Both were subject to heart palpitation, and both horoscopes had indications of heart disease. We find that parents under evil Star Courses at the time their children are born, have transmitted to their offspring peculiarities harmonising with the nature of those Star Courses. Good parents (*i.e.*, parents with good qualities) beget offspring with good qualities and the children have invariably similar aspects to those found in the horoscopes of the parents.

In judging the health and fortunes of a child the student should avail himself, if possible, of the horoscopes of the parents and therein much of the child's physical condition or physical constitution will be found portrayed. We have often observed that when Mars or Jupiter has occupied the fifth house in the father's horoscope, the nature of those planets has been dominant in the nature of some of the offspring. An acquaintance has Mars in the fifth house, and in the case of his son we found the Sun in the ascendant in square to Mars in the Mid-Heaven. The Sun not being otherwise aspected largely imbibed the nature of Mars, making the boy passionate, impulsive, self-assertive, difficult to control and very daring. He also met with accidents. Once, in a fit of passion, he thrust his fist through a glass panel of a door and severely cut his hand, wrist and arm; he was constantly subject to blows and falls. Child and grandfather had identical aspects, *viz.*, Sun in evil aspect to Mars. In the horoscope of his sister we found Mars in the third house in square to the Moon, hence she had all the qualities which emanate from Mars. When the line of ancestry on both sides is wicked, then the offspring will be found to possess sinful qualities, even though the horoscopical qualities may be excellent, the latter can but modify the inherited characteristics. Even so, those who repose confidence in a man, lend him money, etc., because of his good horoscopical qualities, may have bitter cause to regret it, for if bad hereditary qualities are there the person will abuse the confidence and prove very dishonest. Subsequent research has enabled us to add to the subject. We have observed that when Saturn has been found in the fifth house, especially if in adverse aspect to the Sun or the Moon, the children have invariably been delicate. In one case where Saturn was in the fifth house opposed to the Sun, two children succumbed and the remaining three are delicate, one especially so, as she has the Moon in adverse aspect to Saturn. This physical delicacy even descended to a grandchild, who also died in infancy. Not only are physical defects and infirmities inherited; but also mental defects and qualities. Many people have very good horoscopes, even showing a powerful brain and reasoning powers, literary and scientific ability, yet they have inherited but little ability because the quality of the brain inherited has been poor and they have made little headway. Though they have had a happy aspect of Jupiter and Mercury and Mercury and Venus the mental apathy inherited has, so to speak, swamped the horoscopical qualities. Therefore, a good inheritance of brains is of more importance than horoscopical ability. It is, therefore, necessary to know the nature of the hereditary impress ere the astrologer can confidently say if the person will distinguish himself in the world of science, art or literature. We have also found that men with horoscopes indicating no great ability have gone far and accomplished much; but then their parents were clever, consequently the hereditary qualities from gifted parents appear to be greater and more valuable than the horoscopical qualities. We have met persons with Mercury in good aspect to Jupiter, and they have displayed a good deal of stupidity, their parents were doltish, heavy and dull. On the other hand, we have known people with Mercury in good aspect to Venus (which invariably vouchsafes good abilities, literary ability, special aptitude for music and artistic taste), and they have not even studied these subjects. We have found people in obscurity working at a trade for a poor wage, and they have had the finest aspects of Mercury to Jupiter, Venus and Mars. If, therefore, the horoscopical impress does not find an equally good hereditary impress the person will achieve little. The child who comes from clever parents may go far and display genius even if Mercury is in cross aspect to the Malefics, and receiving little or no support from the Benefics. We have found cases where the child's horoscope has given us no clue whatever to the physical weakness, and that child has succumbed to Star Courses which others have easily survived. It was a puzzle to us to account for the early death of the child until we looked up the grandmother's horoscope, when we found that Saturn was in the fifth house, indicating physical weakness, and the death of some of the offspring, consequently in this case both daughter and grand-daughter died. We must, therefore, look beyond the horoscope of the parents of the child, and to the grandparents' horoscopes as well. We must look for the hereditary quality of the impress ere we can arrive at a true estimate of the child's abilities, physical constitution and inherent vitality.

We have found from experience that the hereditary traits of character sway one more in one's acts of life than the horoscopical traits. We have the horoscopes of distinguished writers and clever people in our possession, and these horoscopes do not indicate very superior abilities; but they have inherited qualities quite superior to the horoscopical ones. On the other hand, we have the horoscopes of the children of labourers and poor people; brilliant horoscopes they are with the finest aspects indicative of great mental power, but these men and women display no sparks of genius, they are in very humble walks of life, they are quite ordinary mortals—the result doubtless of a poor inheritance of brains. We could not confidently predict the great artistic ability of Sir David Wilkie if we confined ourselves to the horoscopical significators and the astrologer could not point to any great genius in the horoscope of Sir Joshua Reynolds. He had a good aspect of Mercury and Mars, and Venus and Mars, common enough in the horoscopes of very ordinary people. If the astrologer had had the horoscope of B. R. Haydon when he was a baby he could not have predicted even ordinary artistic ability; but the indications of mental trouble were there. Lord Byron is another example of a bad horoscopical impress, for Mercury is not only opposed to the Moon but also to Mars. Lord Byron's line of ancestry on both sides was strange, eccentric and ill-balanced. The horoscope of W. E. Gladstone does not reveal great mental power, but great eloquence—he was not a philosopher, while the horoscope of George Eliot reveals the finest abilities and exceptional mental power, a well-balanced intellect. If, therefore, the hereditary qualities are equal to those which emanate from the horoscopical positions then George Eliot must have been head and shoulders above her compeers. The horoscope of A. G. Trent certainly reveals exceptional abilities and marked eloquence. The hereditary impress may have been even superior to the horoscopical one since his father was a great scholar, he held an influential position in the British Museum. The astrologer would be by no means confident that he had before him the horoscope of a genius in that of Michael Angelo. Mercury was in good aspect to Venus, the Moon was conjoined with Mercury, aspects which indicated superior abilities; but they are aspects found in the horoscopes of thousands of others who have displayed no great genius. Another great man with one of the finest horoscopes was General Washington, for Mercury was not only in trine to Jupiter but in Sextile to Uranus, to Venus and to Saturn. He won his position through his abilities. It bears a strong resemblance to the horoscope of George Eliot.

Many horoscopes clearly portray that the abilities are the only asset when the Luminaries are badly afflicted and this is why many famous people have been unfortunate pecuniarily and have suffered in health; but they have displayed genius. Swinburne, the greatest of Victorian poets, was born April 5th, 1837.—Mercury was conjoined with Venus and in trine to Jupiter and Mars, in Sextile to Neptune, Semi-sextile to Uranus.

Swinburne, therefore, was truly a genius. Of course, these very fine aspects in the horoscope of Swinburne would enable him to make money; his abilities, therefore, must have been a valuable asset.

Irresponsible writers do much mischief when they say "you have not grasped the main chance because you have hesitated or lacked enterprise."

They tell you that "you have not succeeded because you have not dared, because you have not been determined to succeed, because you have not exercised your will power." They tell you that "your destiny and that of your country is in your own hands," and they ask "what are you going to do with it?" Another writer says "success is the child of audacity," which it certainly is not. It has been our experience to find that more than one person has dared, has speculated, has plunged in his effort to "grasp the main chance"; but his reckless audacity has brought him into the bankruptcy court. One man, after plodding for forty years and accumulating a competence thought after reading such literature that he had been "a bit too slow;" he rose to the occasion and he thought he would "grasp the main chance." He plunged into money commitments in speculation and lost everything, even his forty years' savings. Poor man, he now realises that "success is not the child of audacity." If a man is horoscopically unfortunate the more audacity, the more enterprise and the more plunging into money commitments, the deeper he will become involved.

We were asked the other day why we did not make a fortune on the Stock Exchange. "Alas!" we replied, "the Astrologer with an unfortunate horoscope can no more command success than the man in the street whose horoscope is also unfortunate." Even so, we cannot indicate the rise and fall of stocks. If the Astrologer could do that he could easily become a very rich man.

We were recently severely criticised by an old client for whom we had made some calculations nearly twenty years ago when we were investigating the influence of the newly-discovered planet Neptune. Neptune was afflicting the Sun in his horoscope but we were not sure of this planet's malefic influence, consequently we failed to warn him of the malice of fortune indicated by the subsequent adverse Star Course of this planet. He said that the prognostications were true enough, that he was very successful at certain periods and got money, but why had we failed to warn him of loss at a certain period? "Alas," we said, "when we computed his Star Courses we were unaware that Neptune was a Promittor of evil and it has taken us nearly twenty years to discover that Neptune is a malefic and almost as unfriendly as Saturn when in adverse aspect to the Sun at birth. His adverse aspects to the Moon are not quite so powerful. Subsequent aspects of this Promittor to the Sun have caused heavy money loss, sometimes a serious breakdown in health. Those, therefore, who have had calculations of Star Courses ten or fifteen years ago, when Neptune was omitted from the calculations, should have the horoscope recalculated, for certainly Neptune when afflicting the Sun is a serious menace either to the health or fortunes, according to his position in the horoscope.

Astrology will tell you if you are supported in your enterprise by good planetary authority. It will indicate the most propitious period for taking steps on an unknown road. The interpretation of Star Courses is often very difficult because good and bad Star Courses often coincide; they bring about mutations of fortune, that is to say. when there are good and bad aspects of Promittors or Promissors there is often gain and loss, sometimes much success, but the health suffers. It must always be remembered that the minor aspects, such as the Semi-sextile or Semi-square aspect of a Promittor to the Sun, are more powerfully influential than a major aspect, such as the Trine or Opposition of a Non-Promittor or Non-Promissor.

We have found that Jupiter is almost impotent in the horoscope unless powerfully placed in the ascendant or Midheaven or in Benefic aspect to the Luminaries. If Jupiter is afflicted by cross aspects, especially cross aspects of the Luminaries, his subsequent propitious aspects to them in the Star Courses will not bring good fortune.

CHAPTER II.

SYMBOLS, ABBREVIATIONS AND GLOSSARY OF ASTROLOGICAL TERMS.

(Symbols and abbreviations used in Astrology.)

THE SIGNS OF THE ZODIAC.

Aries	♈	The Ram.
Taurus	♉	The Bull.
Gemini	♊	The Twins.
Cancer	♋	The Crab.
Leo	♌	The Lion.
Virgo	♍	The Virgin.
Libra	♎	The Balance.
Scorpio	♏	The Scorpion.
Sagittarius	♐	The Archer.
Capricornus	♑	The Goat.
Aquarius	♒	The Waterman.
Pisces	♓	The Fishes

THE PLANETS.

Planet	Symbol	Planet	Symbol
Saturn	♄	The Moon	☽
Jupiter	♃	Venus	♀
Mars	♂	Mercury	☿
The Sun	☉	Uranus, or Herschel	♅
Neptune	♆	Neptune	

Also: Dragon's Head ☊ · Moon's N. Node.
Dragon's Tail ☋ · Moon's S. Node.

These twelve signs of the Zodiac are divided and arranged under their different qualities and forms, and it would be well if the student could, from the very beginning, master these various divisions.

♈, ♉, ♊, ♋, ♌, ♍, are northern and commanding signs.

♎, ♏, ♐, ♑, ♒, ♓, are southern and obeying signs.

The northern signs are so-called because they appear north of the equator, whereas the southern signs are south of the equator.

It will be noticed that the signs in the summer semi-circle command, because, during this time, the day is longer than the night. The Chaldeans always considered these northern signs more efficacious and of a nobler nature than the southern signs; hence, probably, the name commanding. In aspect, these signs are in opposition to each other. Example:

Northern.	☍ (opposition).	Southern.
♈	☍	♎
♉	☍	♏
♊	☍	♐
♋	☍	♑, etc.

The Airy Signs are: ♊, ♎, ♒.

These also go by the name of the airy triplicity, and are hot and moist by nature.

The Fiery Signs are: ♈, ♌, ♐.

These are also called the fiery triplicity, and are by nature hot and dry.

These six signs are masculine signs. The fiery signs are in △ to each other, and so are the earthy, airy, and watery signs.

The Earthy Signs are: ♉, ♍, ♑.

They are of the earthy triplicity, and are cold and dry.

The Watery Signs are: ♋, ♏, ♓.

These are by nature cold and moist, and are of the watery triplicity.

These last six signs are also known as the feminine signs.

♈, ♋, ♎, ♑ are cardinal and movable signs.

♉, ♌, ♏, ♒ are fixed signs.

♊, ♍, ♐, ♓ are common signs.

These signs are called fixed, common, and movable, because, whenever the Sun is in one of them, it answers to the season of the year. The cardinal signs are in □ and ☍ to each other, and the same is the case with the fixed and common signs.

♋, ♑ are tropical signs. When the Sun enters ♋ he brings summer to us, and when entering ♑ he brings winter, and *vice versâ* to those in the antipodes. When the Sun is in the beginning of these signs, he turns back from that course to the contrary course. Hence the name tropical. In short, they limit the course of the Sun.

♈, ♎ are equinoctial signs; ♈ begins the vernal equinox, ♎ the autumnal. They are called equinoctial because, when the Sun is in the first point of each, the days and nights are equal.

♊, ♓, and the first degrees of ♐ are bicorporeal signs, or double-bodied signs.

♊, ♌, ♍ (the last only to a certain extent) are barren signs.

♋, ♏, ♓, fruitful signs. They are also called mute. Men born under them are said to be slow of speech.

♋, ♌, ♍, ♎, ♏, ♐, are signs of long ascension.

♑, ♒, ♓, ♈, ♉, ♊, are therefore called signs of short ascension. So called because they ascend in a shorter period of time, the earth being in its diurnal motion, nearly parallel with its orbit, when these signs ascend in the east.

A Table of the Friendships and Enmities of the Planets.

Planets.	Friends.	Enemies.
Saturn	♃, ☉, ☿, ☽	♂, ♀
Jupiter	♄, ☉, ♀, ☿, ☽	♂
Mars	♀	♄, ♃, ☉, ☿, ☽
Sol	♃, ♂, ♀, ☿, ☽	♄
Venus	♃, ♂, ☉, ☿, ☽	♄
Mercury	♄, ♃, ☉, ♀, ☽	♂
Luna	♃, ☉, ♀, ☿	♄, ♂

By the above table it will clearly be perceived, that, according to the ancient astrologers, the friends of Saturn are Jupiter, the Sun, Mercury and the Moon; his enemies are Mars and Venus, and so on with the rest.

Table of the Orbs of the Planets.

	Orbs according to the Chaldeans. Deg. Min.	Orbs according to more modern works. Deg. Min.
♆		♆ 8 0
♅		♅ 8 0
Saturn	10 0	♄ 8 0
Jupiter	12 0	♃ 10 0
Mars	7 0	♂ 8 0
Moon	12 30	☽ 12 0
Venus	8 0	♀ 8 0
Mercury	7 30	☿ 8 0
Sun	17 0	☉ 17 0

The trine aspect of the Sun to ♂, ♄, ♃, ♅ or ♆ is operative when within 11° when applying and 10° when separating.

The quartile aspect of the Sun to ♂, ♄, ♃, ♅ or ♆ is operative when within 11°.

The planets have been found to have much greater power either for good or evil in certain signs. The sign in which a planet is strongest has been called its *house*.

The following table will show the relationship of the planets at a glance:

♈ is the house of ♂, exaltation of ☉, detriment of ♄.
♉   ,,   ♀, ,,   ☽, ,,   ♂.
♊   ,,   ☿, ,,   ,,   ♃.
♋   ,,   ☽, ,,   ♃, ,,   ♄.
♌   ,,   ☉.

♍ is the house of ☿,   detriment of ♃.
♎   ,,   ♀, exaltation of ♄,   ,,   ♂.
♏   ,,   ♂,   ,,   ♀.
♐   ,,   ♃,   ,,   ☿.
♑   ,,   ♄,   ,,   ♂,   ,,   ☽.
♒   ,,   ♄,   ,,   ☉.
♓   ,,   ♃,   ,,   ♀.

N.B.—The opposition of the Sun to ♂, ♄, ♃, ♅ or ♆ is operative when within 12½° of 180°. This we have proved in many horoscopes.

The Fortunes are: ☉, ♃, ♀, also ☽ and ☿, when unafflicted.

The Infortunes are: ♆,* ♅, ♄, ♂ (☿ when afflicted).

Elevated. When planets are above the horizon they are said to be elevated. Those nearest the M.C. are the most elevated.

M.C. means "Medium Cœli" or Mid-Heaven. This is the 10th house.

ASPECTS.

☌ = Conjunction, *i.e.*, when two planets are in the same degree and sign of the Zodiac.

⚺ = Semi-Sextile	30 degrees apart.	Probable orb of	2½° each way.
Semi-Quintile	36 ,,	,, ,,	4°
∠ = Semi-Square	45 ,,	,, ,,	4½ or 5°
✶ = Sextile	60 ,,	,, ,,	5°
Q = Quintile	72 ,,	,, ,,	4°
□ = Square	90 ,,	,, ,,	10°
△ = Trine	120 ,,	,, ,,	10°
⚼ = Sesqui-quadrate	135 ,,	,, ,,	5°
Bq. = Biquintile	144 ,,	,, ,,	4½°
☍ = Opposition	180 ,,	,, ,,	10½ to 12½°†

P., Par., or Par. Dec. = Parallel Declination. An equal distance either North or South of the equator.

Aspects of 22°, 52°, 160° (or round about) are very probably influential.
     22° orb of 2°.
     52° ,, 5°.
     102° ,, 5°.
     155° to 162° with a probable orb of 9° to 10°.

The aspect of 22½° we may call Semi-demi-quartile.
The aspect of 51$\frac{3}{7}$° we may call Septile.
The aspect of 102$\frac{6}{7}$°, Bi-Septile (or 105°).
The aspect of 154$\frac{2}{7}$°, Tri-Septile. (This aspect seems to be operative round about 160°.)

     ° means Degrees of Longitude.
     ′   ,,   Minutes   ,,
     ″   ,,   Seconds   ,,

* Evidence will be adduced proving this planet to be of evil mien.

† Aspects of the Sun to the planets, *i.e.*, an opposition aspect, has an orb of 12½ degrees.

☉ and ☽ are called the lights or luminaries.

Application. The most rapid planet or luminary applying to an aspect or conjunction of another, moving less quickly.

Aspect. A number of degrees; as: ⩗ 30°, ∠ 45°, ✶ 60°, □ 90°, △ 120°, ☍ 180°, also 36° Semi-Quintile.

Angular. A planet is said to be angular when in one of the angles. They are the 1st, 4th, 7th, and 10th houses.

Affliction. A planet is afflicted when in evil aspect with another planet, or if in his debilities; that is, if in a sign in which he has his detriment.

Cadent. A planet in the 3rd, 6th, 9th, or 12th houses.

Cusp. Is the beginning of any of the houses, as measured by the Sun.

Detriment. Should a planet be in the sign which is opposite to the sign forming its own house, that planet is said to be in its detriment. Example: ♈ is the house of ♂, therefore its opposite sign, ♎, would be its detriment should Mars be posited therein.

Dignified. A planet in its own house is said to be essentially dignified.

Dignified accidentally. This consists of a planet being well placed in the heavens either in the angles or otherwise. The strongest accidental dignities are the 1st and 10th houses; then the 7th and 4th, 9th and 3rd.

Declination. Same degree of declination north or south of the equator; that is, the same distance north or south of the equator.

Aspects and probable approximate Orbs: the point or degree at which aspects become operative. The exact point or distance at which an aspect ceases to be influential or begins to be operative cannot be accurately defined. It will be observed that the opposition aspect has a tremendous length of orb.

Conjunction Sun and Planets, Moon and Planets when within 10 degrees.
Semi-sextile about 28 degrees to 32 degrees.
Semi-quintile (36 degrees) 34 degrees to 38 degrees.
Semi-square 40½ degrees to 49 degrees.
Sextile 55 degrees to 68 degrees.
Quintile 68 degrees to 76 degrees.
Square 80 degrees to 99½ or 100 degrees.
Trine 109 degrees to 130 degrees.
Sesqui-quadrate 130½ degrees to 139 degrees.
Bi-quintile 140 degrees to 149 degrees.
Opposition 168½ degrees to 190½ or 191 degrees.
Parallel is operative within one degree of declination.

New aspects approximate length of orbs of aspects of **Sun and Moon to the Planets**.

Semi-demi-quintile 17 degrees to 19 degrees (good).
Semi-demi-quartile 20 degrees to 24 degrees (bad).
Septile 50 degrees to 53 degrees (good).
Bi-Septile 100 degrees to 104 degrees (good).
Tri-Septile 156 degrees to 158 degrees, or 160 or 165 degrees. (We think this is a good aspect.)

The aspects however do not overlap; the trine may reach an orb of 130°, but it cannot go beyond that point, as it would reach the orb of the □.

Exaltation. When a planet is in a very powerful dignity it is said to be exalted. (See Table of Planets with their Houses and Exaltations.)

Mundane Aspects. Are formed from distance in the world in semi-arc, wholly independent of the Zodiac. Thus the distance from the 10th house to the 12th house is a sextile aspect. A planet on the ascendant is in square to the M.C., the nadir, and in opposition to the 7th house. Mundane quartiles and oppositions are intensely evil, whilst mundane sextiles and trines presage good fortune. Mundane parallels are an equal distance of two planets from any angle.

Orb. The word is now used to describe the distance at which a planet may operate from a partile aspect (partile means the same degree; thus ☿ in 6° 20′ ♈ would be in partile aspect to ♀ in 6° 20′ ♊). (See Table of Orbs among the Signs.)

The Orbs of the Planets.

The orb is the point of influence, when a planet begins to be influential.

The word orb signifies the distance of one planet from another (to which it is applying or separating, approaching or leaving), and at which it becomes influential, or ceases to have effect. Example:—Suppose Venus were in the 21st degree of Taurus and the Moon in 8° of the same sign, the latter would be approaching the conjunction of Venus and would be within orb when she reached the 11th degree of Taurus. When a planet is within 6° of the cusp of any house it is then on the cusp of that house. An aspect may be said to be influential when the luminaries are within 10° of each other or of the planets, and 7° may be said to have effect in planetary aspects; that is, the conjunction or aspect of one planet to another, such as a sextile of Mercury and Mars, a trine of Jupiter and Saturn, etc. To find out when two planets, or a planet and a luminary, are within orb, add the sum of their orbs together and divide by two.

For instance: the orb of Saturn is 8°, the orb of Jupiter 10°; these added together and divided by two would give 9°. But we do not consider a distance from one planet to another planet within aspect or conjunction when outside 7°, though the Chaldeans allowed a longer orb; indeed, they allowed an orb between the Moon and Jupiter to have effect inside 12°, and that of Jupiter and the Sun at 14°.

The minor aspects such as the 22° may only have an orb of 2½°. The 30°, 36° and 45°, an orb of 3½°. The 52° and 104° may have an orb of 5°, 6°, or a little more. But it is really impossible to indicate the exact point or degree at which the influence ceases. The Sun's opposition aspects have an orb of 12½°.

The major aspects such as the 120° may be operative slightly beyond 10° when the aspects are formed by the Sun with ♃, the ☽ with either ♃ or the Sun.

Oriental. East.

Occidental. West.

Peregrine. A peregrine planet is posited in a sign where it has no essential dignity of any kind.

Promittor. That which promises an event. ♄ and ♂ in evil aspect to the Sun pledge bad fortune. ♃ and ♀ assure good fortune, when in good aspect to the Sun or Moon.

Retrograde. When a planet is going backward as from ♉ to ♈.

Reception (Mutual). Two planets being found in each other's houses will be in mutual reception, as ♂ in ♐ (the house of Jupiter), and ♃ in ♈ (the house of Mars).

Significators. Lords of the ascendant or 1st house (thus should ♐ be on the cusp of the 1st house, then Jupiter would become lord of that house). The lord of the 10th would be significator of his honour and business. Planets in the ascendant, or 1st house, are also significators.

Separating. Planets having been in aspect, and just separating, as, ☽, ☌, ♂ in 5° ♈, the moon would be separating when in 6° ♈.

Triplicity. A fourth of the Zodiac, or an equilateral triangle.

Weak signs. ♋, ♑, ♓, because when one of the signs is on the ascendant, the child is less robust. That is to say, his constitution and vitality would not be so good as a person born with Aries, Taurus, Scorpio, or Sagittarius on the ascendant. For instance, those born under Gemini, Libra, or Aquarius, are said to have much strength of constitution.

Zenith. The point directly overhead.

Zodiac. A circle of twelve signs of the ecliptic 18° broad.

Orbs: Applying and Separating.

The aspects which are close are more powerful than those which are only just within orb of the aspect, when either separating or applying.

The orb of the ⚺ or 36° the semi-quintile is $2\frac{1}{2}°$, but it means that the aspect is operative when the planets are $2\frac{1}{2}°$ short or $2\frac{1}{2}°$ beyond the 30° which is the ⚺ or 36° which is the semi-quintile. Suppose the Sun was 168° from ♂, it would be within orb of the opposition. Suppose the Sun was 192° from ♂ it would be just within orb of the opposition aspect. Suppose the Sun was 108° from ♄ it would be within the orb of the trine aspect. But if they were 130° apart the trine has gone and a sesquiquadrate is forming.

Thus a trine aspect has an orb when the Sun is applying of quite 11° or a little over since the point of influence begins at 108° but when separating the orb is cut at 130°, thus when the aspect is applying its orb is 12°, but when separating it is 10°, *i.e.*, an orb of 10° on one side and 12° on the other.

CHAPTER III.

EXPLANATION OF THE TWELVE HOUSES OF HEAVEN AND THEIR ASTROLOGICAL SIGNIFICATION.

THAT the student may form a clear idea in his mind of what is meant by the twelve houses of heaven, let us suppose the whole celestial globe or sphere of heaven to be divided into four equal parts by the horizon and meridional line; now each of these into four quadrants and each quadrant into three equal parts, by lines drawn from points of sections in different parts of the horizon and meridian, at equal distances from each other. By this operation the whole globe or sphere will be divided into twelve equal parts, which are called the twelve houses of heaven. The lines thus drawn will make the following figure. The space in the centre (were the figure drawn in circular form) might represent the space wherein the earth moves; but we generally write the name, day, year and hour of the person's birth whose horoscope is to be calculated.

These twelve houses are, as will be seen from the above, either angular, succedent or cadent.

The angular houses are four, called:—ascendant, mid-heaven, the 7th house, and the bottom of the figure, or 4th house. These were deemed the most powerful, influential and fortunate by the Chaldeans.

The succedent houses (11th, 2nd, 8th and 5th) were supposed to come next in force and virtue to the angles, and the cadent houses (3rd, 12th, 9th and 6th) were considered of the least efficacy or weakest of them all.

Modern astrologers consider the 1st and 10th houses the strongest. Planets placed therein, according to them, would have great influence over the native throughout his life.

Next in power they place the 7th and 4th; less powerful are the 9th and 3rd; the weakest are the 6th and 8th.

But, indeed, each house has its effects and more or less influence on the native and the circumstances of his life.

The 1st house betokens the personal appearance and disposition, life, mind and character. Planets posited therein bear the most powerful influence upon the life and destiny of the native. Saturn or Mars in this house never fail to give accidents or indisposition, trouble, and a chequered career; while Jupiter and Venus therein, free from cross and opposition aspects, prefigure good health and fortune and a happy life.

The 2nd house relates to wealth or property, prosperity or adversity, loss or gain. Saturn in this house, for instance, especially when in cross aspect to the Sun or Moon, causes pecuniary difficulties, losses of money;

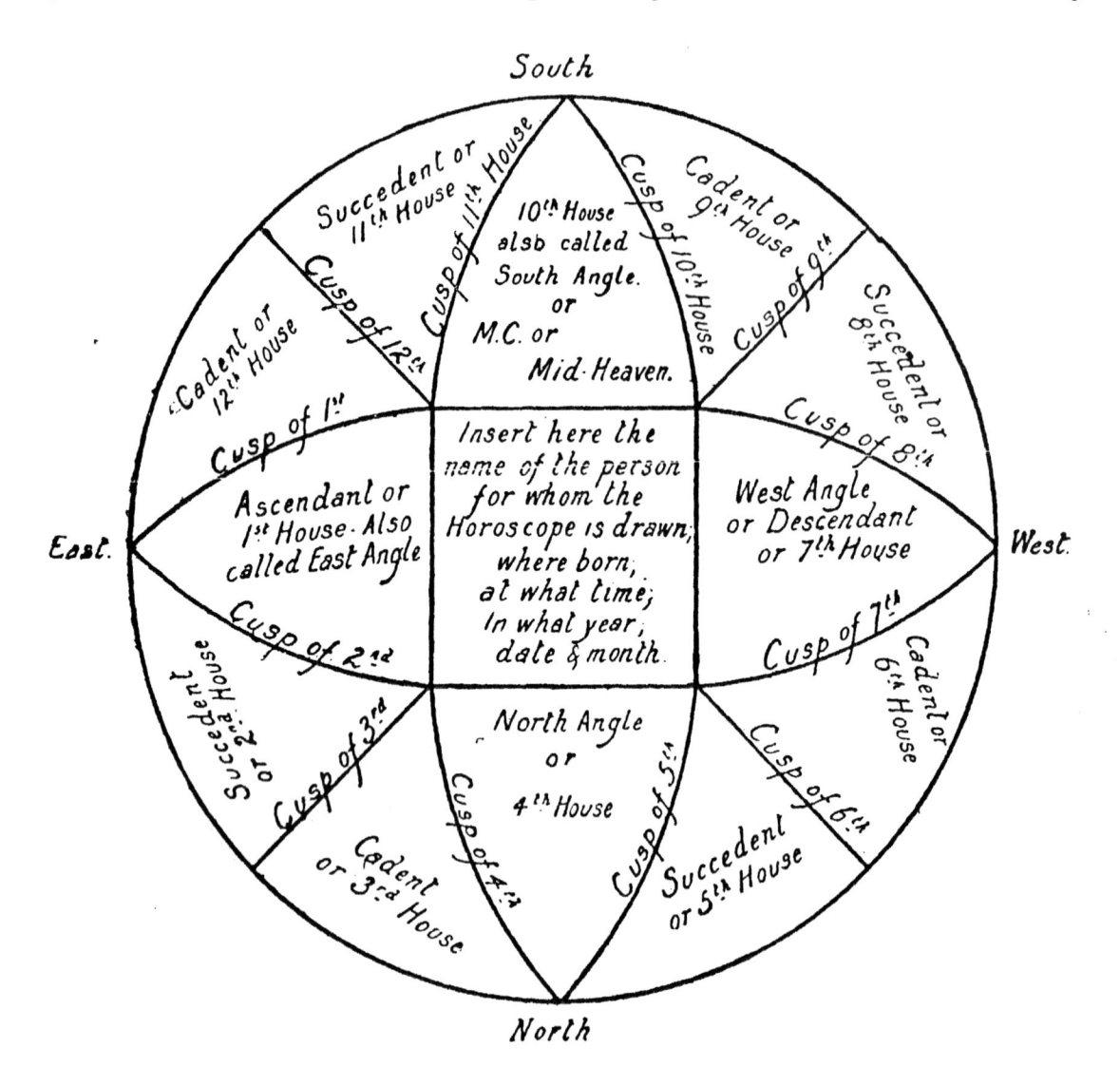

A FIGURE OF THE HOROSCOPE OF THE TWELVE HOUSES.

whilst Jupiter therein is a constant source of wealth; Mars there, would cause losses by rash enterprises.

The 3rd house relates to brothers, sisters, relations, neighbours, short journeys and writings. Planets in this house influence the mind greatly. The Chaldeans read from this house the condition of kindred and of brethren. The Moon therein is a pregnant source of journeys; Saturn and Mars there, cause trouble from kindred, neighbours and short journeys. It is the house of mutations, according to Zael (a Chaldean writer).

The 4th house prefigures the father of the native, his own property and inheritance; it also indicates his position and condition at the end of life. Mars in this house causes trouble between the native and father; while Saturn there, indicates trouble in the eventide of life, sickness to the father; the acquisition of property if this planet is strong and well aspected, but loss if the contrary. It relates to the father's patrimony.

The 5th house. All predictions relative to offspring, speculations, gaming, lotteries, etc., are formed from this house. It is the house of pleasure, enjoyment and merry-making of all sorts.

The 6th house. This is associated with servants, cattle, sickness, diseases, Saturn in this house, conjoined with the Sun, would lower the vitality considerably, causing sickness and weak constitution; it brings trouble from servants and inferiors.

The 7th house signifies marriage, description of wife or husband, partnerships, law suits, public enemies, opponents, public offices. Mars in this house causes domestic infelicity; Saturn there, indicates trouble, and delays marriage or prevents it altogether; Jupiter or Venus there, portray the best of husbands and wives, superlative happiness and felicity in marriage, success in public dealing, if unafflicted by malefics.

The 8th house. This shows the nature of death; it also relates to legacies, wills, property of the native's partner in marriage. Mars or Saturn there, cause loss and trouble concerning wills or the goods of the dead; whilst Jupiter in this house vouchsafes legacies and hereditaments.

The 9th house tells us of the safety and success of long journeys either by sea or land; religion, dreams, preferments, etc. When a planet is in this house it has great influence on the mind of the native; for instance, Saturn there, adds gravity, reserve, fear of the unknown and reverence for Divine things; the native often becomes religious if Jupiter is posited therein, for this planet adds sincerity of soul, a serious spirit and the strongest regard for equity, the native is conscientious.

The 10th house. This being the M.C. or meridian, and so most elevated part of the heavens, resolves all questions concerning persons in power and authority; it represents the native's mother, and has signification of honour and preferment (whether attainable or not), employment or profession, business and success therein. Saturn or Herschel in this house causes discredit in many ways; Jupiter there, vouchsafes honours and distinction.

The 11th house. Of friends, hopes and wishes; the friends correspond to the nature of the planets therein. Jupiter here, brings many good friends, sincere—who contribute to one's happiness and good fortune; Mars and Saturn there, for instance, cause bad friends, who cause trouble and disquietude.

The 12th house. Called by the Chaldeans the house of tribulation, affliction, anxiety of mind, trouble, distress, imprisonment; it is the house of secret foes, backbiters, and of assassination, suicide, treason, and in fact misfortunes.

CHAPTER IV.

PROBABLE DESCRIPTION OF PERSONS PRODUCED BY EACH OF THE SIGNS WHEN ASCENDING AND NO PLANET THEREIN.

Aries—♈. This sign ascending at birth produces a person of small stature, lean body (unless it be in the first part of this sign, which would then make it more fleshy), strong, large bones and limbs; a swarthy or sallow complexion, with sandy or light coloured hair and piercing eyes. The disposition is determined and impulsive. The nature of this sign inclines the native to anger, but makes him witty, ingenious and of quick perception. Saturn or Mars therein would alter it for the worse, whereas the effect of Jupiter or Venus would be for the better.

Should a sign be strongly occupied by planets, these would entirely change its nature and effects; otherwise each sign would unalterably follow its own nature.

Mars is the ruler or significator of the Aries person.

Taurus—♉. Signifies a person of short, thick-set stature; full face, dark curling hair and a swarthy complexion. The disposition would be somewhat unfeeling, impulsive, self-assertive, confident, injudicious, slow to anger, but when roused, violent and furious as a bull and difficult to appease; swayed by passions, likes and dislikes. It is the sign of self-appreciation, and Venus is the ruler or significator thereof.

Gemini—♊. The person defined by this sign would be tall and straight, with long arms but short hands and feet; rather dark complexion, with a bright and lively expression in fine eyes of a dark hazel colour. This sign gives good mental attributes, excellent understanding and great fluency of speech; it makes the natives judicious in worldly affairs, temperate, receptive in mind, highly intuitive, and very unlikely to go to extremes in anything. They are children of moderation. Mercury is the ruler or significator.

Cancer—♋. Indicates a person of small or short stature, the upper part of the body being generally larger than the lower. The face is round with a pale sickly complexion, brown hair, grey eyes. The Cancer person is mild, gentle and sympathetic; the Moon is the ruler or significator. The disposition would be unstable and inconstant, timid, and void of energy. The constitution weak and effeminate; if a woman, she may have many children.

Leo—♌. This is a regal, commanding and eastern sign; the only house of the Sun, and as such is by nature hot, dry, fiery, masculine and barren. The native of this kingly sign is generally of a good full stature, with broad, square shoulders.

One of the characteristics of the Lion is an austere countenance, with large, commanding eyes, a fearless and sprightly glance which becomes fierce under provocation; the face is oval and complexion ruddy or sanguine, with dark or yellow flaxen hair. The disposition is open, bold, courteous, firm, ambitious, and quick in judgment; the heart generous, the mind aspiring and lofty with a resolute and courageous spirit. The Sun is the ruler or significator.

Virgo—♍. This sign in the ascendant gives the native a stature somewhat above medium height with a well-formed, slender body; a round face, complexion ruddy brown, with lank hair of a black or dark brown colour; the voice is thin and shrill. The disposition is studious but lacking in firmness, the mind witty and ingenious.

Should this sign ascend with Mercury therein, free from the malevolent aspect of Saturn and the Moon in ♋, the native would make an excellent orator. Mercury is ruler or significator.

Libra—♎. Produces a tall, well-made body; round and lovely face with a fine sanguine complexion and grey eyes; the hair long and lank of a yellow or flaxen colour. In old age the face will be full of pimples or of a deep red colour. In disposition, friendly and affable. Though with self-esteem the mind will be just and upright, amiable, with conversible power and independence of character; specially intuitive. Venus is ruler or significator.

Scorpio—♏. Prefigures a strong, robust and corpulent body of middle stature, with short neck and legs; a broad face, brown complexion and brown curling hair; secretive and not to be trusted—capable of dissimulation; these people are never straightforward. The subject will be reserved and thoughtful in conversation, but deceitful; a veritable Talleyrand, unfeeling, and often abrupt; unrefined, inelegant, coarse, without any sympathy, if Mars has an evil aspect to Mercury. Mars is ruler or significator.

Sagittarius—♐. This sign rising in a natus endows the native with a well-formed, strong and active body, somewhat above the middle height; face rather long, handsome and comely; ruddy complexion and chestnut hair. Such a person generally makes a good horseman; is intrepid, courageous and careless of danger. He is generous, free and good-hearted, with regard for honour and rectitude. Jupiter is the ruler or significator.

Capricorn—♑. The house of Saturn and the exaltation of Mars is a four-footed sign and of the earthy triplicity. It is a cold, dry, melancholy, feminine, nocturnal, movable, cardinal, domestic and southern sign. Persons born under this sign are of a slender stature and not very well-formed, with long, thin face and neck, dark hair, narrow chest and thin beard. The disposition is sharp, witty and subtle; selfish and covetous; often sensitive and nervous. They are capricious and impressionable. Saturn is the ruler or significator.

Aquarius—♒. This is the house of Saturn and of the airy triplicity. It makes a well-set, stout and robust person with a somewhat long, pale and delicate countenance; clear complexion, bright sandy or dark flaxen hair. The disposition is kind-hearted; a gentle and even temper, with a scientific turn of mind; evenly balanced, firm, sociable and constant. Saturn is the ruler or significator. Some modern writers say that Uranus is the ruler or significator.

Pisces—♓. The twelfth sign is of the watery triplicity. It is a cold, moist, feminine, phlegmatic, common and fruitful sign. It is the house of Jupiter, and in it Venus is exalted. The native would be of a short, thick stature, round shouldered; with pale complexion and brown hair. The nature of the sign does not tend to a robust temperament. It gives a slothful disposition, inactive, easeful, and lacking the energetic principles and physical activity. The physical condition is often a clog to mental action. They lack the self-assertive and aggressive power and are too easy-going. Jupiter is ruler or significator.

CHAPTER V.

PROBABLE DESCRIPTION OF PERSON PRODUCED BY THE DIFFERENT PLANETS ASCENDING IN EACH OF THE SIGNS.

How welcome are sign-posts when one is travelling in a strange land or driving along unknown country roads!

Remember that the following rules alone will not always describe the person.

In trying to find out or describe personal appearance, due regard must be taken of all other testimonies, and in this the student cannot be too careful.

He must not only study the ascendant and the planets therein, but also the sign occupied by the lord of the ascendant.

Again, should two planets be in the ascendant, it would considerably alter these descriptions, or there might be a planet in the 1st house, but it might not be in the sign on its cusp. In that case he would have to study the ascending sign and the sign occupied by the planet.

All pros and cons must be studied; every iota of information well balanced, analysed and compared.

This requires great discernment and good judgment, but with care and patience all things are possible.

SATURN—♄.

Saturn is an evil and malignant planet—the star of sorrow, melancholy and disappointment; when in, or opposing the mid-heaven, he threatens loss of honour and misfortune. Of course, his good aspects to the Sun, Moon and Jupiter mitigate the evil and bring this world's goods in abundance.

♄ is productive of the best disposition in ♒, and about the worst in ♓ and ♋. In ♉ the native is bad, given to drink, and malicious. In ♍ and ♑, fretful, crafty, inquisitive, discontented and fanciful. In ♏ or ♓ a Robespierre, a double-faced, cruel and cowardly person.

When ♄ occupies the mid-heaven or 4th house and afflicts one or both the luminaries, then the malice of fortune is certain. In general those born under this sad planet are of a solitary nature, fond of retirement, the funereal and deep mysteries; they are mournful and often commit suicide, if Saturn is in evil aspect to Mars and the latter planet is in the ascendant.

The student will sometimes find the early degrees of Leo on the ascendant, and Saturn in that sign in the 2nd house.

Probable Description of a Person produced by ♄ ascending in each of the signs.

♄ *in* ♈. Medium height, lean and well made, ruddy complexion, high forehead, large, full eyes, dark hair, little beard; in character this person will be ill-natured, quarrelsome, boastful, self-conceited, cruel and revengeful if crossed in his purposes.

♄ *in* ♉. Indicates one of small stature, lean, ill-made, dark hair. He is generally inclined to be vicious, revengeful and given to all sorts of dissipations. The most ignoble of men is the Saturn in Taurus person; he is a treacherous, cowardly fellow and untrustworthy; one who vows vengeance and would stab in the dark.

♄ *in* ♊. Rather above the middle height with a well proportioned body; the face oval, hair either black or dark brown; of an ingenious and humane nature, somewhat perverse, unfathomable and subtle, generally unfortunate.

♄ *in* ♋. Signifies one of medium height, thin, and sometimes crooked or ill-made; the constitution sickly, the face thin with brownish hair; in his behaviour he will be deceitful and malicious, of a cunning nature, and much given to drink and vicious actions; heavy and dull.

♄ *in* ♌. A somewhat noble bearing of middle stature, broad shoulders and large bones, the hair a light brown; the temper would be passionate and malicious; the person is given to boasting, but lacking in courage, and really not so noble and bold as he looks; the courage is more apparent than real.

♄ *in* ♍. A tall and spare body, swarthy complexion, black or brown hair; this person would be rather melancholy, fond of learning, malicious, inclined to be dishonest, unforgiving, reserved and subtle.

♄ *in* ♎. Represents a tall person with a handsome and well-formed body, oval face, broad brow and brown hair; high spirited, self-conceited, antagonistic, selfish, fond of argument and soon moved to anger, independent, proud and opinionated.

♄ *in* ♏. A short stature, thick set, black or brown hair; arrogant, quarrelsome, apt to be mean and base in his actions; in fact, a mischief maker of the worst kind; if Mars is in evil aspect to Saturn, he is a wicked man.

♄ *in* ♐. Handsome, well formed person of middle stature, with brown hair; in his behaviour, courteous to all (though rather irascible and hasty), obliging and forgiving.

♄ in ♑. A rather lean person of medium height, long face, sallow complexion, black or brown hair; he is avaricious, melancholy, grave, discontented, peevish, not easily pacified in anger; most revengeful and double-faced, if Saturn has the cross aspects of Mars.

♄ in ♒. Denotes a person of middle stature, rather inclined to be stout, black or brown hair; a lover of arts and sciences, of a courteous disposition, but very conceited; a person of much ingenuity and sometimes of genius; prudent and shrewd.

♄ in ♓. Middle stature, pale complexion, and black or dark brown hair; a most malicious, contentious, sottish person; deceitful in his dealings; deliberate and yet fickle in his actions; antagonistic, severe and untrustworthy.

Note.—In reading these descriptions the student must remember that the fortunate planets, by their propitious rays, modify the otherwise baneful influences of the malevolent stars.

JUPITER—♃.

This planet, when auspicious (*i.e.*, in the mid-heaven or ascendant, and in good aspect to the luminaries and planets), gives "every earthly good and every perfect gift," and is equally powerful for good as Saturn is for evil.

In the earthy signs he makes the native rather proud and selfish; in the fiery and airy signs his good nature and sincerity of soul are great facts; in the watery signs, and receiving cross aspects, the native is a boon companion, devoted to social functions, wasting his substance, fond of approbation, vain and sometimes pedantic.

The child of Jupiter has generally a fine carriage, a commanding presence, with a genial and optimistic temperament.

Probable Description of a Person produced by ♃ ascending in each of the signs.

♃ in ♈. Produces one of middle stature, oval visage, ruddy complexion, brown or flaxen coloured hair, with sharp sight; an obliging person of free and noble disposition, a lover of friendship and peace; if near violent and fixed stars it renders the person rash and fickle.

♃ in ♉. Medium height, swarthy complexion, brown hair; wise, discreet, humane, kind-hearted and sympathetic; of a good carriage and a lover of the fair sex.

♃ in ♊. A well-formed, tall body above the middle height, sanguine complexion, brown hair; a lover of arts and science, delighting in ladies' society, courteous, frank and obliging.

♃ in ♋. Of medium stature, oval face, pale complexion, dark brown or black hair; thoughts somewhat aspiring, aiming at great things; a busybody, conceited, but well-disposed; a great lover of the other sex.

♃ *in* ♌. Portrays one of a tall stature and a well-proportioned body, light coloured or yellow curling hair, ruddy complexion; of a good disposition, just, generous, free and courteous, delighting in manly and heroic actions, courageous, desirous of honour, and quick to resent an injustice.

♃ *in* ♍. Generally a handsome, well-composed person, brown or black hair; he is ambitious, covetous, boastful, a lover of money, of a hasty disposition and certainly not generous; much given to the study of arts and sciences.

♃ *in* ♎. Designates a tall, well-made person, oval and pleasant countenance, light brown or flaxen hair; the disposition is very good, delighting in all pleasant recreations, free, generous and obliging; a most attractive person.

♃ *in* ♏. Medium stature, compact, well-built body, brownish hair; the native is conceited, ill-natured, covetous, arrogant, ambitious and industrious.

♃ *in* ♐. A tall, upright, well-formed body, oval face, ruddy complexion, hair of a chestnut colour; in disposition just, noble, perfectly trustworthy, with the strongest internal consciousness of right and duty; a lover of horses and a good horseman.

♃ *in* ♑. Short stature, thin face, pale complexion, brown hair; this person will be delicate in constitution, peevish, desponding and ill-natured (if Jupiter is afflicted), of a mutable nature and inconstant in attachments; if Jupiter is well aspected, the disposition is good.

♃ *in* ♒. Denotes a person of well-set, middle stature, good complexion, brown hair; a pleasant, merry disposition, delighting in good company, just, merciful and of an amiable nature; a great favourite and always much appreciated; personality attractive.

♃ *in* ♓. A mean stature, inclined to stoutness, light brown hair; studious, good-hearted and very ingenious, a lover of mirth and music, constant in attachment and affectionate; generally fortunate in travelling by water.

MARS—♂.

Mars t'a frappé de son tonnerre
En mille aventures de guerre.

Mars, the fierce god of war, is the cause of anger and of all that is actively hostile, violent and contentious in the world.

The influence of Saturn may be compared to a "prolonged and lingering adversity; that of Mars to a quickly malignant fever, quenching its thirst in the life-blood of its victim." When ill-dignified or afflicted the life of the ill-starred child of Mars often ends violently, and at times hangs on the stiffness of the trigger of the gun and its resistance to the pressure of the human hand.

The native is bold, extremely determined, headstrong, independent and desperate; very adventuresome and often the pioneer of new enterprises. The child of Mars is subject to aggressive fortune, rather than disappointments and the malice of fortune of the Saturnine child. The Mars man must do or die.

Probable Description of a Person produced by ♂ ascending in each of the signs.

♂ *in* ♈. Indicates a well-set, big-boned person of middle stature, swarthy complexion, curling hair (sometimes red or of a light colour), hazel eyes, with a sharp, bold, confident glance; a bold, courageous, masterful disposition, fond of ruling and war; austere, quick in anger and combat. warlike and proud.

♂ *in* ♉. Medium stature, inclining to stoutness, dull complexion, broad face and features, black hair; this person has often a mark of some weapon on his face; he is treacherous, deceitful, frequently vicious and profligate; ill-natured. If Mars is near the Pleiades he is unfortunate.

♂ *in* ♊. Tall, well-proportioned person, black or brown hair; a wandering, unsettled mind; with an irascible, rash and turbulent nature; ingenious, but not fortunate.

♂ *in* ♋. Short, not well-proportioned stature; in fact, often deformed; dull, white complexion, brown hair; this native will be of a sottish and oppressive disposition; fond of drink and quarrelsome, bad tempered and servile, ignoble, capable of meanness, unfortunate through his own actions, often unmannerly and rude.

♂ *in* ♌. Portrays a tall, well-made body, endued with health and strength; big face, large eyes, dark, flaxen-coloured hair; the disposition hasty, choleric, generous, noble, and fond of outdoor sports; very firm, but not ill-disposed. He will vaunt and is a lover of warlike pursuits.

♂ *in* ♍. A well-proportioned stature of medium height, swarthy complexion, brown or black hair, hasty in anger, unforgiving and irritable; the native will be revengeful, conceited, hard to please and unfortunate in his undertakings. The student should also notice if Mars is well aspected by ♃, ☉ or ☽, as this would considerably alter the significations for the better.

♂ *in* ♎. A rather tall, well-made body, oval face, cheerful and pleasant expression, sanguine complexion, light brown hair; this person will be ambitious, quick in anger, conceited and boastful, amiable, fond of dress and cheerful.

♂ *in* ♏. Well-set person of medium height, swarthy complexion, broad face, black curling hair; clever in arts and sciences, of good abilities, but of an ungrateful, revengeful, cruel, quarrelsome and deceitful disposition; a man of subtlety and penetration, he is clever but not good.

♂ *in* ♐. Denotes a tall, well-proportioned person, oval face, very good complexion, brown hair; in disposition hasty, but generous and free, delighting in warlike pursuits, fond of good and merry company; high-minded, jovial, courageous, loquacious, fond of approbation and of applause, a good disposition; those who would propitiate him must applaud him.

♂ *in* ♑. Short, lean stature, thin face, small head, bad complexion; in mind very ingenious, quick-witted, courageous and high-minded, possessing, on the whole, a good disposition. The native is generally fortunate and happy in most of his undertakings, penetrating, with a deductive judgment, shrewd, and sees more of his environment than most people; he is discreet (unless Mars is afflicted) and has great determination —a contriver, of skilful capacity; men of ability and discernment have ♂ rising in ♑.

♂ *in* ♒. Medium and well-proportioned height, good complexion, red or sandy-flaxen hair; quarrelsome, fond of argument (in which he will seldom get the best), of a turbulent nature, generous and quick to forgive, soon provoked and soon appeased; his want of prudence tends to ill-fortune.

♂ *in* ♓. Short, fleshy, badly composed stature, light brown or flaxen coloured hair, bad complexion; this is a deceitful person of a dull and stupid understanding, dissembling, indolent, artful, sottish, sensuous and untrustworthy—an uncertain quantity—a man of artifice and pretence, shifty and covert.

THE SUN—☉.

> By his magnetic beam he gently warms
> The universe, and to each inward part,
> With gentle penetration, though unseen,
> Shoots genial virtue even to the deep.
>
> MILTON.

The Sun is the giver of life, for did the Sun disappear from the heavens, all life would cease without his beneficent and life-giving rays.

This planet in the ascendant prefigures a person with great force of character, immense physical power, commanding presence and individuality.

When well aspected or dignified, *i.e.*, in ♌ or ♈, the native is noble, humane and a faithful person, with the strongest consciousness of integrity; he will scorn to take an advantage over an opponent; quick tempered and resentful of the least impertinence in the fiery signs, wilful and difficult to bias in the earthy signs.

☉. When in ♒, ♎, or if afflicted, the child of Sol is unfortunate; if ill-dignified the native is more submissive, a tyrant and often a sycophant, seeking self-aggrandisement, with generosity more apparent than real, pompous and pedantic.

The Sun is the significator of credit, honour and dignity. The Solar man inspires confidence because he is a tower of self-confidence, self-assurance and self-reliance. His belief in himself inspires this confidence in others.

Probable Description of a Person produced by ☉ when ascending in each of the Signs.

☉ *in* ♈. Denotes a strong, well-formed, middle stature, good complexion, light flaxen hair; in disposition lofty, noble and generous, even to his enemies, spirited and an independent character; he delights in war and generally gains honour and renown therein. If the Sun is in good aspect to Mars, the native is a man of valour and victory.

☉ *in* ♉. A short, well-set person, broad face, dull complexion, wide mouth, large nose, brown hair; he is proud, bold, self-confident, fond of strife, and has a great idea of his own opinions with exaggerated self-importance.

☉ *in* ♊. Well-formed body, large stature, sanguine complexion, brown hair; this person does not easily take offence, and is of a courteous, affable disposition, even-tempered, mild, kind-hearted, and sometimes imposed upon by others through a too confiding, unsuspicious nature.

☉ *in* ♋. An unhealthy person of small stature, bad complexion, brown hair, sometimes with a defect in the face; he is a jovial and boon companion, delighting in all kinds of sports and pastimes, good-natured, pleasant and generous, harmless, cheerful, lacking executive power, and fond of the other sex.

☉ *in* ♌. This planet in his own house gives a well-proportioned, strong body, full face, sanguine complexion, light or yellow hair, fine, large, expressive eyes; the native will be proud, noble, faithful, just, and true to his promises, disdaining mean or sordid actions; a lover of good and pleasant company, of commanding appearance; ambitious of honour, magnanimous, fond of authority, and easily susceptible to indignities.

☉ *in* ♍. A tall, well-proportioned stature, rather slender, an abundance of brown or black hair, good complexion; a pleasant, ingenious, scientific person of a good disposition though rather austere; cheerful, convivial, fond of recreations.

☉ *in* ♎. Describes a person of upright and erect carriage, oval visage, good complexion, full eyes, light coloured hair; he is proud, extravagant, apt to be unfortunate and exposed to much danger, especially in war; he often falls short of his aspirations; the mind is honourable and the disposition good.

☉ *in* ♏. Square, well-set person of middle stature, dusky complexion, fleshy face, brown hair; of a rugged, ingenious nature, clever in war, opinionative and antagonistic; ambitious, overbearing—a man of honest bluntness.

☉ *in* ♐. Represents a tall, well-set, comely person of sanguine complexion, oval face, light brown hair; the native will be high-sprited, proud, ambitious of honour, lofty and noble in disposition, scorning to take a mean advantage, fond or sports; austere, aristocratic, a man who delights in philanthropy.

☉ *in* ♑. Small, ill-proportioned stature, thin, spare body, oval face, pale complexion, brown hair; just, witty, ingenious, of an undaunted spirit and fond of ladies' society; good-natured, though often hasty, reasonable and good-tempered.

☉ in ♒. A well-composed, corpulent body, of medium height, full, round face, good complexion, light brown hair; proud, ambitious, fond of ruling, but well-disposed; ostentatious, free from vindictiveness and rather vain; the disposition is good.

☉ in ♓. A person of low, stout stature, round face, pale complexion, light brown or flaxen hair; if a male, he will be a lover of the other sex, fond of sports, a spendthrift and prodigal; otherwise inoffensive, often effeminate, extravagant and intemperate; a man of indulgences.

VENUS—♀, THE RESPLENDENT, MIRTH INSPIRING.

The radiant star of beauty and of love's young dreams.

When Venus is in the ascendant and unafflicted the native is sweet-tempered, graceful, engaging, fascinating, affectionate, with little will power; possessing much tenderness, refinement, love of social pleasures; attractive in personality.

When afflicted, the person is sensuous, amorous, dissipated, easily succumbs to temptations and to over-indulgence.

The qualities generated are according to the aspects she receives.

The children of Venus are the rays of sunshine which light up the dark valleys of our existence; they incline us to the merry side of life, alluring us away from the grave and the serious, for the moment, with their irresistibly winning ways and love of fun.

Probable Description of a Person produced by ♀ when ascending in each of the signs.

♀ in ♈. Portrays a slender, fairly well-proportioned body, of middle stature, good complexion, light hair; as Venus is in her detriment in this sign, the person may be indiscreet in his acts; he will be of a restless nature and a lover of company, often pensive, mutable and uncertain, lacking tenacity.

♀ in ♉. A handsome, well-shaped person of medium height; the native is good-natured, obliging, a general favourite with everyone, fond of singing and dancing, humane, mild and even-tempered, winning and kind-hearted.

♀ in ♊. Slender, well-made body, good complexion, brown hair; tender-hearted, honest and just in all his actions, kind to the poor, sympathetic and loved by all; mild, inoffensive and gentle.

♀ in ♋. Short, rather fleshy stature, round, pale face, light coloured hair; indolent, fickle and fond of drink, inconstant, often slothful and lacking energy.

♀ *in* ♌. Moderately tall person with a well-proportioned body, good complexion, round face (sometimes freckled), full eyes, light brown or sandy hair; in character—conceited, proud and passionate; but free, generous, forgiving, good-humoured, sociable, soon angry, but soon appeased.

♀ *in* ♍. Stature of medium height, well-formed body, dusky complexion, oval visage, dark brown or black hair; an ingenious person of an active, subtle mind, with an inquiring inclination after knowledge; eloquent, aspiring, with conversible power and seldom fortunate.

♀ *in* ♎. A well-proportioned, tall, upright figure, oval face (with dimples in the cheeks and sometimes freckles all over the face), sanguine complexion, pretty brown hair; the native is courteous, obliging, most amiable; a lover of good and virtuous company, generally well-beloved by all.

♀ *in* ♏. Describes one of middle stature, well-set, rather fat, broad face, dark complexion, dark brown or black hair; a quarrelsome, envious and hateful person; often vicious, succumbing to temptations and unworthy actions, in short, a person of evil propensities.

♀ *in* ♐. Tall, well-made person, oval face, clear complexion, light brown hair; of great moral courage, noble spirit, free and generous in disposition, somewhat proud and passionate in anger, but soon over; fond of recreations, kind-hearted, good-tempered, an obliging, fortunate person, full of generous impulses.

♀ *in* ♑. Indicates a person of middle stature, spare body, thin face, pale and sickly complexion, dark brown or black hair; in character, conceited, fond of drink and a great boaster; often indiscreet, making rash changes to his detriment, greedy as to diet and fond of women.

♀ *in* ♒. Gives a handsome, well-proportioned body, very good complexion, light brown or flaxen coloured hair; very good disposition, courteous, obliging, a lover of peace, gentle, affable, and one who will eschew evil; humane, fortunate in his or her affairs, and much appreciated by friends.

♀ *in* ♓. A person of medium height, round face (and sometimes a dimple in the chin), good complexion, brown or flaxen coloured hair; of an ingenious wit, just in his dealings, a lover of peace and quietness; altogether a nice disposition; mild, good-humoured, but lacking tenacity, which will make the native unstable.

Mercury—☿.

This planet is the source of wit, ingenuity, skill in art and sciences.

When well dignified in the ascendant (especially in ♊, ♍, ♒, ♎, ♑) and free from quartile and opposing rays, the mind is vigorous, active, receptive, tenacious, intellectual, aspiring, highly intuitive, eloquent; the native may become eminent through his abilities. In the fiery signs the person will be hasty, sharp, quick with his tongue; in ♉ and ♑ finesse reaches craft, selfishness, fondness for the good things of this world; he will be opinionative and vindictive. In ♊, ♍, ♎ and ♒ he is penetrating and sagacious with more than the average acuteness, and the abilities are enhanced if ♃, ♀, ♂, ♄ or ♅ assist ☿ by good aspects.

In ♏ this planet produces foxishness and diplomacy approaching deceit; when afflicted by the malefics the native is capable of much mischief and of an evil temper.

Should ☿ be afflicted by ♂ or ♄, the native partakes of their malignant natures, for Mercury is receptive and acquires the nature of planets aspecting him; therefore the native's disposition will absorb all this.

☿ in the ascendant and Saturn in trine aspect thereto would make the native born at that moment, reticent, careful, sane, dejected, fretful, peevish, murmuring, perverse; whilst an aspect of Mars in lieu of Saturn would have the opposite effect, adding courage, self-assertion, self-esteem, (the martial combative spirit), enterprise, confidence, rashness—a striking contrast to the fearful, hesitating Saturnine aspected Mercurial man. Jupiter's good aspect to Mercury adds wisdom, probity, rectitude, purity and goodness; the faculty for acquiring knowledge, a superior discernment, sagacity and penetration, making the native generous, tolerant, indulgent and trustworthy. Jupiter is the source of virtue, uprightness, wit, nobility and eloquence.

The aspects of a kindly Venus to Mercury add elegance, tenderness, sensuousness; the gentle, pleasing, merry and sunny nature we all love. They are wise, these fun-loving children, because they make the best of life, rejecting the sombre for the vivacious. They are equally as devout, with all the reverence for the Divine possessed by their brethren of Saturn with sad countenance; prudent, just, susceptible to the beautiful, the artistic, music, singing; they have eloquence and often literary gifts—Chesterfields in politeness and courtesy.

An aspect of Uranus adds surprising penetration, a singularly open and receptive mind, which is creative; rejecting the conventional paths trodden by others. The native is capable of generating ideas, impressions from observation and phenomena. Because of these traits of character he is invariably dubbed eccentric, and certainly he is irregular and erratic in his way of study; but his singularity saves him from a tedious routine and the contracted views of the parrot-crying man—parrot-crying because they but voice the opinions of others, while the Uranian man is a path-finder; a student and never a babbler.

Probable Description of a Person produced by ☿ when ascending in each of the signs.

☿ *in* ♈. Produces a short, thin, slender body, oval face, swarthy complexion, light brown hair; a discontented person, witty, clever, self-assertive, impulsive, highly impressionable, ambitious, restless; an orator with conversible power.

☿ *in* ♉. One of middle stature, well-set, corpulent body, swarthy complexion, dark brown hair; fond of company and the other sex, lazy and loving his own ease, with a keen appreciation for good fare; self-indulgent, often indolent.

☿ *in* ♊. A well-made, tall person, good complexion, light brown hair; the native will be ingenious, intellectual, cultured, possessing good taste and a good mind for the study of arts and sciences; a good disposition, quick, active and very clever.

☿ *in* ♋. Represents a person of short stature, thin face, bad complexion, sharp nose, small, expressionless eyes, dark brown hair; he will be malicious, fickle, given to stealing and lying; an uncertain quantity, with great finesse and a sharp tongue; a dissembler.

☿ *in* ♌. A large stature, swarthy complexion, round face, large eyes, light brown hair; a haughty, proud, mischief-making person of a contentious disposition; vaunting, lofty and choleric.

☿ *in* ♍. Tall, slender, well-made figure, long face, dark complexion, brown or black hair; fond of dress, ingenious, of a scientific and literary turn of mind, subtle and careful of his affairs; well-disposed and generally an accomplished person; Mercury unafflicted makes a good orator.

☿ *in* ♎. One of a moderately tall, well-composed stature, sanguine complexion, light brown hair; this person will possess a good disposition, be thrifty, ingenious, just, virtuous; fond of learning and all scientific subjects; an equitable person.

☿ *in* ♏. A middle stature, well-set, strong and able body, dusky complexion, dark brown curling hair; this is a wit with few good qualities, fond of company and women; malicious, selfish, subtle, ill-disposed; he has an eye to "number one."

☿ *in* ♐. Rather tall, well-made, ruddy complexion, oval face, large nose, brown hair; quarrelsome, contentious, and, indeeed, his own and worst enemy; the learning in this case is often mere pretence; his passion is soon appeased, he is hasty in judgment to his detriment.

☿ *in* ♑. A person of short stature (sometimes bow-legged), thin face, muddy complexion, light brown hair; often sickly; of a peevish and fickle disposition, sharp, active, acute and penetrating, easily perturbed, often complaining.

☿ *in* ♒. An indifferent stature, corpulent, fleshy body, full face, good complexion, brown hair; the native is of a scientific turn of mind, of great wit, often interested in occult subjects, very ingenious; a student, open-minded and sociable; usually beloved by his friends; with that intellectual ability which accomplishes much.

☿ *in* ♓. Low stature, sickly, pale complexion, thin face, brown hair; a drunkard, sometimes wasteful, indolent and peevish, often disconsolate, ambitious of honour.

The Moon—☽.

Cynthia, the Queen of the Heavens.

The Moon is variable, partaking of good or evil, according as she is aspected by good and evil stars.

When angular and unafflicted in a nativity, she gives great success in life and continual good fortune. Her ☌, ✶ or △ to Jupiter are exceedingly fortunate, making the native prosperous in acquiring this world's goods.

In the watery signs, ♋ and ♓, the person is much appreciated; but all this depends upon the aspects she is receiving, for the disposition is not good if the Moon be afflicted by Mars or Saturn, or even ♀.

The good aspects of Venus and Jupiter, on the other hand, add the best of qualities and beget the most attractive of personalities.

Probable Description of a Person produced by the ☽ ascending in each sign.

☽ *in* ♈. Describes a person of well made, medium height; round face, good complexion, light brown hair; in temper changeable, churlish and choleric, versatile, restless, mutable and often passionate; ambitious of honour.

☽ *in* ♉. A well-set, strong, corpulent body, middle stature, black or dark brown hair; the disposition is sober, obliging, gentle and just; the person is much liked, being very amiable, attractive in personality, and good-tempered.

☽ *in* ♊. One of tall, well-proportioned stature, good complexion, dark brown hair; this is a deceitful, crafty, ill-natured, subtle person of a very ingenious mind.

☽ *in* ♋. Well-proportioned, rather fleshy, middle stature, pale complexion, round face, dark brown or black hair; a pleasing and kind disposition, just and wise, good-natured and candid; the native is indulgent, inoffensive, rather lacking in resolution, versatile, but singularly free from passion.

☽ *in* ♌. This seldom proves a fortunate person. The stature is large, body well-made, full face, large eyes and light brown hair; the person will be proud, ambitious, domineering, of lofty airs, consequential, hating to be under subjection to anyone and beloved by few; a man of self-importance.

☽ *in* ♍. Portrays a person of large stature, indifferent complexion, long face, black or dark brown hair; a pensive and ingenious nature; but covetous, imposing, miserly, selfish, loquacious, often melancholy and seldom fortunate.

☽ *in* ♎. Moderately tall and well-made person, sanguine complexion, light brown hair; a nice disposition, very amiable, fond of music, dancing, and all recreations; much appreciated by the other sex, eminently fitted for social functions.

☽ *in* ♏. A short, and often fat, person, pale, dark complexion, black or dark brown hair; malicious, treacherous and covetous in disposition, conceited, ill-conditioned or ignoble; such people gain little love from their neighbours and have a great liking for drink.

☽ *in* ♐. Well-formed, middle stature, sanguine complexion, oval face, light brown hair; in temper, hasty but forgiving; a passionate, ambitious, but obliging person, lacking tenacity of purpose, free-spirited, aiming at great things.

☽ *in* ♑. Low stature, body and face spare and lean (often with some defects in the knees), brown or black hair; the native will be selfish, idle, indulgent, and indeed have few good qualities; a servile creature, mean and often sensuous.

☽ *in* ♒. Defines a middle stature with a well-made, rather corpulent body, sanguine complexion, brown hair; this person has an inventive nature, and is of a courteous, ingenious and good disposition; the personality is attractive; delighting in recreations, and abhorring low and evil deeds.

☽ *in* ♓. Short, rather obese stature, pale complexion, bright brown hair; an indolent, sottish person, easy-going, with some sensuousness, and susceptible to gaming and drinking.

If the Moon be well aspected it mitigates her evil significations, and this holds good for all the planets.

Uranus or Herschel—♅.

This planet's nature is said to be peculiarly independent and original, eccentric, inventive, impressionable. The French describe its nature as *outré*—being out of the common, *i.e.*, odd, queer. The person born under this planet is erratic, singular, impressionable, studious; often disdaining the forms and methods of others—an oddity certainly.

Probable Description of a Person produced by ♅ *ascending in each of the signs.*

♅ *in* ♈. Defines a well-formed stature, medium height, rather slender, sanguine complexion, fair hair; the disposition fitful, changeable, ambitious very impressionable, with much self-esteem.

♅ *in* ♉. Short stature, rather corpulent, pale complexion, darkish hair; an unrefined nature, obstinate, boastful, and malicious.

♅ *in* ♊. Moderately tall figure, well-built, fair complexion, light brown hair; ingenious, ambitious and subtle in disposition; intuitive, generally clever and fond of scientific subjects.

♅ *in* ♋. Low stature, sanguine complexion, darkish brown hair; quick to take offence, but soon forgives; wayward, impulsive, rather fond of drink, lacking tenacity of purpose.

♅ *in* ♌. Middle stature, light brown hair, fair complexion; possessing self-importance, exaggerated pride; a little stubborn and arrogant.

♅ *in* ♍. Medium height, fairly well built, thin body, brown hair; the native will be ingenious, with a taste for sciences and literature; eccentric, impressionable, miserly and malicious. We have observed that such people are quick at learning, quiet, reserved, adopting a line of their own, and fond of searching for curiosities; hasty-tempered, taking no notice of others and never led by them.

♅ *in* ♎. A tall, well-made person, fair hair, pale complexion; this is a person of great precision and will-power, aspiring, proud, sensitive and fond of sciences; if aspected by ♀ and ☿, ♅ gives good abilities.

♅ *in* ♏. Medium height, well-built person, dark complexion and hair; a most undesirable acquaintance, malicious, crafty, unreliable, fond of drink, sometimes most dangerously aggressive if provoked.

♅ *in* ♐. Well-made person, fair complexion and hair; candid and generous, energetic, fond of recreations; a man often swayed by impulse.

♅ *in* ♑. A small darkish person, not well-formed, dark or pale complexion, dark brown hair; selfish, vindictive, fickle and malicious; with great ideas of his own abilities.

♅ *in* ♒. A person of medium stature, fair complexion, brown hair; impressionable, studious, penetrating, eccentric, prudent, intelligent, and often fond of studying sciences.

♅ *in* ♓. Short, not well-formed stature, palish complexion, brown hair; often cast down and indulgent, not intellectual; easy-going and pleasure-loving; a man of little wit.

CHAPTER VI.

THE NATURAL QUALITY, INFLUENCES AND EFFECTS OF THE PLANETS.

Herschel—♅. This planet is malefic and the evil which emanates from him is often peculiar, strange and unexpected.

His nature is eccentric and he is especially inimical to marriage; if in the 7th house or afflicting the Moon in a male's horoscope, constant domestic infelicity is indicated.

The planet is hostile to love and the fair sex. When conjoined with or afflicting the Sun in the natus of a female, he delays marriage and causes sad divisions.

The planet's eccentric nature makes him an uncertain quantity, and benefits from his good aspects are generally unexpected, sudden, peculiar and extraordinary. The child of Herschel is romantic, original, penetrating, often dogmatic, critical, fond of occult things. The traits of character emanating from Herschel are mystical, psychometric, psychological, observative; such as marvellous perceptive powers which baffle the judgment of readers of character.

Saturn—♄. The malevolent planet, Saturn, represents a person of middle stature, broad shoulders, with small thighs and legs; a dark swarthy or pale complexion with leering, often dark eyes; lowering brow, thick nose and lips, large ears, black or dark brown hair and thin beard. There is often a palish, ghastly look about the child of Saturn.

As significator of travelling he betokens long, arduous journeys and perilous adventures. When well dignified (*i.e.*, well aspected and in airy or fiery signs), the person signified by Saturn will be of an acute and penetrating understanding; thoughtful and sober, managing all his concerns with discretion. In his conduct he will be austere, rigid, laborious, ungenerous, patient and mindful of injuries. He is fond of old associations; if he loves he will be constant; if he hates it will be to the death.

As a rule the Saturnine person is a selfish miser and grasping for this world's goods. When ill-dignified or afflicted the native will be covetous, envious and miserly; of a dissembling, crafty and malicious disposition; perpetually dissatisfied with himself and his surroundings; base, sordid, cowardly, stubborn and treacherous.

The lowering looks, cloudy aspect, seemingly melancholy temperament, austere expression, reserve and gravity, the close and covetous, the laborious, patient slowness, the malicious spirit, (mindful of injuries) the vindictive principles, the sordid, base, cowardly and suspicious, the envious and treacherous, the repining gloominess, the nervous fear and mistrust are all traits of character of the Saturnine person when in the ascendant and in cross rays to the other planets and luminaries. The Saturnine person is more sullen if the planet be in earthy signs, for there he is double-faced, waspish, and will never look thee in the face; there is then a melancholy, mournful ring in his voice. His moroseness often drives him to suicide— Such is the funereal demeanour of the child of Saturn.

Jupiter—♃. This so-called "Greater Fortune" is a masculine, temperately hot and moist, airy and sanguine planet. He rules the lungs, liver, blood, and digestive organs.

The person described by this planet should be robust, of an erect, tall figure, well-set and handsome body, short neck, broad chest, strong thighs and legs, long feet.

The face oval, with a rosy complexion, high forehead, large grey eyes, soft and thick brown hair.

Jupiter makes the native temperate, modest, wise, affable, good, magnanimous, frank, benevolent, sober and just. If well-dignified, he gives charming manners and an admirable disposition; the person will be upright in all his doings. If ill-dignified, *i.e.*, ill-aspected, the person will be prodigal, plunging into excessess and dissipation, pandering to his superiors, reckless, easily led astray, immoderately luxurious, honest only in appearance; a boon companion, given up to every humour.

The child of Jupiter, when he is well-aspected, is generally tall, fair, handsome, portly, erect, free in his carriage, noble in appearance, gracious in aspect, dignified and magnanimous, just, good, affable, with the strongest internal consciousness of right and duty; mild and temperate in manners. The nature of this planet is that of freedom, confidence, generosity, frankness, benevolence, charity, goodwill, nobility of soul. Attractive in personality, open faced—the reverse of the cunning, mistrustful, reticent, malicious, deceitful Saturnine nature. The children of Jove are happy members of society, faithful and constant in attachment, aspiring to honour, incapable of mean or sordid actions.

Mars—♂. This fiery planet (the lesser infortune) is the first above the earth, and is a masculine planet; in nature, hot, dry, choleric and fiery. He rules the gall, left ear, head, face, imagination, and is the author of strife and dissensions.

Mars represents an active, intrepid person of short stature, well-set, strong body (rather lean than fat), with large bones.

A bold and confident countenance, brown, ruddy complexion, red or light brown hair, sharp hazel eyes.

When well-dignified the native will be courageous, daring, careless of danger, if he may but triumph over his enemy; prudent in his private affairs. He is fearless, irascible, of an unsubmitting nature; eager for battle with pen or sword, though not lacking in generosity and magnanimity, he will at the call of duty face the cannon's mouth bravely. When ill-dignified, he might commit murder or become a robber, and will delight in quarrels. The native is then prone to violence and wickedness; he is rash, unbending, rude and ferocious.

The disposition will be cruel, unjust, rash and treacherous, fearing neither God nor man; far from fortunate, but not so evil as Saturn, for his influence is by no means so lasting. The influence of Saturn may be compared to " a lingering disease," and that of Mars to " a burning fever."

The real desire of martial persons is martial glory, and they frequently die in battle. The life of the child of Mars is constantly " under the sword of Damocles." The death shafts of Mars are swift and sure. The combined cross rays of Mars and Saturn, when either are in the ascendant, beget a Nero, an Ali Pasha, or a Marat.

Moon—☽. Denotes a person of large stature, inclined to be stout and phlegmatic (especially if oriental), with short arms, thick hands and feet; round face, pale complexion, grey eyes.

If occidental, the native will be thin and ill-formed, and if she be in conjunction, square or opposition Sun at the time of birth, she leaves a blemish in or near the eye.

If well-dignified, the disposition will be kind, tender, timid, well-intentioned, sociable, fond of novelties, company, travelling, and of engaging manners.

The native is unstable through versatility, sympathetic, disliking discord; a good comrade, and capable of close friendship.

If ill-dignified, she represents an idle, drunken person, hating work of any kind, and mean-spirited. When the Moon is in the ascendant or 1st house, the native partakes of the influence not only of the Moon herself, but of the planets in aspect to her; if ill-aspected, her influence is malevolent, and propitious if well-aspected. Her aspects to Jupiter and Venus add generosity and kindness of heart, tenderness, amiability, sympathy and excessive good-nature. The good aspects of Mars add courage, will power and force of character; the bad aspects of this planet add hardness, rashness, wilfulness, stubbornness and austerity. When in good aspect to Saturn, a careful, economical, persevering, firm, self-willed, cautious, wary, plodding spirit is vouchsafed; whilst the cross rays of Saturn to the Moon beget a taciturn, suspicious, mistrustful, reserved, mean, unhappy, melancholy temperament. The aspects of Uranus (good or bad) are those of eccentricity, of wayward traits of character, impulsiveness, sensuousness. The native is troubled in mind under the bad aspects, and in body often by some peculiar disease.

Venus— ♀. Venus, the lesser fortune and author of mirth and pleasure, is a feminine planet, temperately cold and moist.

She inclines to early love engagements and makes a handsome, well-formed person, though not tall unless she be oriential, when the stature would be tall and stately; if occidental, short and stooping, but comely.

Round and beautiful face, fine complexion, lovely dark or blue bright eyes, and light coloured hair.

When well-dignified she gives a quiet, friendly disposition, naturally inclined to neatness, excelling and delighting in music. Accomplished, winning, vivacious and fun-loving almost to a fault. Amorous, but virtuous.

This planet, ill-dignified, represents a riotous, profligate person; one who will have little regard for his or her reputation.

As the significator of journeys, Venus promises pleasures, profits and safety.

The child of Venus has a fascinating personality, and love at first sight is frequently due to the bewitching, enchanting, irresistible influence of the eyes; as Charles Lever sings:—

> "And as sages wise of old,
> From the stars could fate unfold;
> Thy bright eyes, my fortune told,
> Lady, lady, mine!"

Refinement, ideality, artistic taste, delicacy, high caste, vivacity, love of gaiety and social enjoyments, literary, musical and artistic talents, the soft and the effeminate, warmth of affection, all emanate from an unafflicted and well-aspected Venus in the ascendant or house of life.

Mercury—☿. Mercury, the least of all the planets, is by nature cold, dry and melancholy; he is either masculine or feminine, lucky or unlucky, and his influence for good or evil depends upon his position in the heavens, and how he is aspected by good or unfortunate planets.

He denotes a tall, straight, spare stature, with long slender arms, hands, fingers, and feet; narrow face, straight nose, thin lips, brown complexion, hazel or chestnut hair and very little beard.

In an oriental position, the stature will be shorter, hair sandy, and complexion somewhat sunburnt and sanguine.

If occidental, the complexion will be sallow, with deep sunken eyes.

When well-dignified in a natus, the person will be extremely witty, an excellent orator, of a subtle imagination and retentive memory; his powers of persuasion will be great, and his understanding almost incomparable.

If the planet be ill-dignified or ill-aspected, he will be incapable of acquiring any substantial learning, but will have a high opinion of his own abilities, a shallow mind, and an indiscreet tongue.

The Mercurial person is mischievous, when the planet receives the cross or opposition rays of Mars or Saturn; he pretends to more learning than he often possesses. A good aspect of Jupiter and Venus, or Uranus, would endue the native with genius, and the cross aspects would beget eccentricity.

"For great wit to madness nearly is allied."

Such positions would give mental activity, fluency of speech, sagacity, great acuteness and penetration, reasoning powers, philosophical judgment, the mental subtlety of the metaphysician, mathematical ability, craft and diplomacy, a receptive mind, an impressionable sharpness and great intuition.

The Sun—☉. The most powerful of all the planets is the life-giving Sun. He is by nature masculine, hot and dry, but more temperate than Mars.

When he presides at a birth he makes the native large, bony, and strong of body, with straight and well-proportioned limbs, sallow, sunburnt complexion, large, high forehead with light or sandy curling hair, fine hazel eyes, full and piercing.

If well-dignified, the person will be proud, magnanimous, firm, generous and lofty in disposition. The solar man is not of many words, but when he speaks it is with confidence and to the point; he is usually thoughtful and reserved, humane, kind-hearted, and even affable. In friendship faithful, sincere, and true to his promises. His deportment is stately, and he is a lover of magnificence. His mind is above anything base or sordid, scorning mean or dishonest acts, words or deeds. He is born to rule, quick in anger, and resentful of impertinences.

But, when this powerful planet is ill-dignified, the disposition will be proud and arrogant in the extreme; the understanding shallow; the mind restless, opinionative, and headstrong; the heart will be prone to cruel and ill-natured deeds, if ill-aspected by Mars or Saturn.

When the Sun is in the ascendant, and in good aspect to Jupiter, the native is above all things, faithful and sincere, a philanthropist, and incapable of dishonourable actions. In short, a noble soul, with honour, candour, and rectitude.

The Dragon's Head—☊, *and Dragon's Tail, or Cauda*—☋. These are neither signs nor constellations, but only the nodes and points wherein the ecliptic is intercepted by the orbits of the planets, and particularly that of the Moon, making with it angles of 5° 18'.

The Head of the Dragon is masculine, partaking of the nature of both Jupiter and Venus; but the tail is feminine and in direct opposition to the qualities of the Head.

Lily says: "The Head of the Dragon is considered of a benevolent nature and almost equivalent to one of the fortunes; when in aspect to the evil planets it is found to abate their malignant efforts to a very considerable degree. But the Dragon's Tail we have already found of an evil tendency. When joined with evil planets their malevolence is doubled; when with good, their beneficial influence is much diminished."

The Dragon's Head in the 10th house is indicative of good fortune. Cauda, or the Dragon's Tail, on the mid-heaven is inimical, and causes discredit and mutations of fortune, especially if near malefic planets or opposed or ill-aspected by them.

The Moon's nodes are found in the Ephemeris, and their movements are retrograde at the rate of about 3m. per day.

Probable Description of the Person produced by ♅ ascending in each of the Signs.

♅ *in* ♈. Begets a well-formed person, moderate stature, complexion sallowish. Self-assertive, wilful, forceful, of a stirring, pushful nature.

♅ *in* ♉. Short stature, broad, thick, palish complexion; unruly and unsubmissive; therefore ungovernable, indulgent.

♅ *in* ♊. Well-built, tall, fair, ingenious, intellectual, penetrating; a clever and active person.

♅ *in* ♋. Well-set, not tall; fairish complexion; kindly, rather reticent, indulgent; still, quickly resentful.

♅ *in* ♌. Middle stature, broad, large head. Complexion fair or ruddy. Lofty, confident, free and open, impartial, sincere. In fact straightforward.

♅ *in* ♍. Sometimes tall, well-made, darkish complexion, clever; with love of science, art, and literature; vindicative in spirit, impressionable.

♅ *in* ♎. Rather handsome, fair, tall. Careful, evenly balanced, punctilious, highly-strung; a person of some exactness, fond of literature; tender-hearted but proud and sensitive.

♅ *in* ♏. Thick stature, dark. Subtle, reticent, not innocent of guile; a person of some dexterity, capable of artifice and of feigning and acting a part.

♅ *in* ♐. Tall, well-built, handsome. Complexion fair or ruddy. Generous, impartial, open-hearted, equitable, honest and guileless, fond of sports.

♅ *in* ♑. Of low stature, not well-built, of a darkish complexion. Acquisitive, touchy, versatile, easily perturbed and susceptible to affronts; designing and subtle, but not ill-disposed.

♅ *in* ♒. Rather tall, well-made, broad; fair complexion. Intelligent, careful, discerning, not assertive but reticent and peace-loving.

♅ *in* ♓. Low in stature, light complexion. Easy-going, comfortable, demulcent, slow, tranquil, and not easily ruffled. Indeed, the serene, sedate temperament is not easily disturbed by passion.

The Influence of Neptune—♆.

It has taken us nearly twenty years to acquire some knowledge of the influence of Neptune. We find that this planet, when in adverse aspects to the luminaries, is an evil promittor and produces the malice of fortune in whatever house of the heavens he is found. If he is in cross aspect to either the planets or luminaries, he will cause mischief and misfortune. If in adverse aspect to the Sun, his power is the greater for evil. When he promises misfortune he never fails to bring it in a subsequent aspect to the Sun. But this planet's good aspects to the Sun certainly bring a modicum of good fortune. The good aspects of ♆ to ♃ bring gain by will or by marriage, and often an independence from one of these sources. When ♆ is found in good aspect to the Sun, the houses which hold the Sun and Neptune will indicate the benefits to be expected. For instance, if the ☉ or ♆ is in the 9th house, these would indicate gain by a long journey; if in the 10th much success, or a powerful position in some firm—a good post with a good stipend. If the ☉ or ♆ be in the 2nd house then money will be acquired. When in adverse aspects to the luminaries and posited in the houses, Neptune presages the following:

In the 1st. He assails the health.

In the 2nd. He causes money loss, and much difficulty in making money.

In the 3rd. He causes loss through journeys, neighbours and kindred.

In the 4th. He causes loss in connection with property, lands and mines.

In the 5th. Heavy loss in speculation or through offspring.

In the 6th. Loss through servants and employees, also infirmities and ill-health, which are impediments to success.

In the 7th. Domestic infelicity, often separation or divorce.

In the 8th. Trouble in connection with wills, the goods of the dead, or marriage partner's substance.

In the 9th. Adverse fortune on journeys and voyages.

In the 10th. Discredit, sometimes bankruptcy.

In the 11th. Loss by friends.

In the 12th. Others work mischief, treachery is to be feared.

Neptune— ♆.

We have found that this planet is a malefic, and produces the malice of fortune, when in cross aspect to the luminaries. When found in the 7th house, he often prevents marriage in the horoscope of a female; in the horoscope of a male he causes domestic infelicity. The woman who has Neptune on the western angle in her horoscope will either remain single, or find misfortune in marriage and an early widowhood. When this planet afflicts the Moon in any part of the horoscope, then misfortunes will come to the native. When afflicting Venus, he causes disappointment in love.

The Sun in quartile aspect to Neptune is the promissor of disaster, forty-five years later, at the sesqui-quadrate. If Neptune is in the 2nd house, then bankruptcy is to be feared.

Jupiter in good aspect to Neptune, he promises inheritances or gain by will; whilst the evil aspects indicate a paucity of money, difficulty in getting money.

Neptune's good aspects to the luminaries help the native to a competence. If in the 5th house and in evil aspect to the luminaries, then heavy loss in speculation is threatened.

The good aspects of Neptune to Venus, Mercury, and the mid-heaven, impart talents and abilities.

We have not observed that the evil aspects formed by Neptune to the Moon are so powerfully adverse as the adverse aspects formed by this planet with the Sun. When ♆ is in ☌, ∠, □, ☍, ⚼ with the Sun, then he will be a menace to health and fortune, that is to say, he will cause heavy losses, a serious breakdown in health.

CHAPTER VII.

THE PLANETS IN THE HOUSES.

The Effects of Uranus in each of the Twelve Houses.

In the 2nd. Changes in monetary affairs. If afflicting either of the luminaries, heavy losses and bankruptcy may be the result; in any case, mutations of fortune.

In the 3rd. Many changes and much unsettledness, especially if aspected by the Moon. The influence of Uranus in this house, is great, especially on the mind, and, if aspected by Mercury, gives good abilities. In fact, the planet has a peculiar influence on all things connected with this house, such as letters, writings, neighbours and relations. It also inclines to the occult studies.

In the 4th. Disagreements with parents; trouble with property or inheritance, and, unless well-aspected, misfortunes in life's eventide.

In the 5th. No offspring, if in barren signs; loss in gaming or speculating; if aspected by the Moon or Venus, too much given to dissipation, which often brings disgrace.

This position is never good for the attainment of a high moral character. Uranus in this house, afflicting the Moon, produces sensuality in the nativity of a male.

In the 6th. Troubles from servants, and, if afflicting the Sun or Moon, some peculiar disease is to be feared.

In the 7th. An unhappy marriage, if any. This is bad for public undertakings, partnerships and dealings with lawyers. The position delays marriage.

In the 8th. If ill-aspected, a marriage partner poor in worldly goods; troubles with legacies, and, if afflicted, the native loses them. Subsequent evil aspects of the Sun to Uranus often cause early death, if within orb of the aspect at birth.

In the 9th. If aspected by Mercury, the native will be clever; if by the luminaries, he will have changes. The planet in this house influences the mind greatly; expect evil in all things connected with this house, if Uranus be badly aspected.

In the 10th. Mutations in honour, credit, esteem, and employment; troubles with superiors, employers, and changes in the vocation; often sudden losses in business, if afflicting the Sun.

In the 11th. Inconstant friends, and if afflicted, they may ruin the native by a pretended friendship. If well-aspected, help from friends.

In the 12th. Secret enemies and jealousy.

THE EFFECT OF SATURN IN EACH OF THE TWELVE HOUSES.

In the 2nd. Troubles in all monetary matters, and losses especially when ♄ is afflicted by the luminaries. If well-dignified and unafflicted, success with landed property, income therefrom.

In the 3rd. Misfortune in travelling, or through neighbours, brethren and relatives, with letters and writings. If he aspects the Moon or Mercury the native will be suspicious, stubborn, jealous and cautious to excess.

In the 4th. If afflicted, the father suffers in health, and survives not many years. If undignified or ill-aspected, a miserable and poor eventide of life. If well-aspected or dignified, the contrary; the native will probably inherit and have lands and property bringing him in gold, which he will carefully hoard.

In the 5th. This position is bad for speculation and sports of any kind. If ill-aspected, sickness or death of offspring, but especially when he afflicts the luminaries.

In the 6th. Bad servants, losses through them and much sickness, especially if in bad aspect to the luminaries; in common signs, weak chest and lungs; in cardinal signs, chronic indigestion and disordered system; in fixed signs, bladder troubles, heart disease or syncope, and often chronic rheumatism.

In the 7th. A selfish, cold, melancholy, reserved marriage partner; bad for partnerships, lawsuits and public dealings; more so if afflicting the Sun or Moon. The wife or husband delicate in health, and the marriage seldom proves a happy one; it delays or prevents marriage.

In the 8th. Probably a partner of little substance; trouble with legacies and wills. If well-aspected and well-dignified, the trouble will be mitigated, and there might even be gain in these matters; the partner might then possess money.

In the 9th. He strongly influences the mind, making the native more or less fearful, cautious, reserved, with inclination for religious beliefs; if afflicting the luminaries, unfortunate and dangerous long journeys. Great suspicion, taciturnity and maliciousness when afflicting the Moon, particularly if the latter is in the ascendant; it often causes strange dreams and visions.

In the 10th. If dignified and well-aspected, some success in business; when ill-aspected, disgrace, losses and trouble. If afflicting the Moon, sickness and ill-fortune to the mother.

In the 11th. False friends, unless well-aspected; if ill-aspected, injury from them.

In the 12th. Many secret enemies, and if ill-aspected, the native will suffer through them; he has to fear false accusations and imprisonment.

The Effect of Jupiter in each of the Twelve Houses.

In the 2nd. Prosperity and success in wealth, especially if the planet is strong and essentially dignified and well-aspected; if afflicted, little gain, and money difficulties.

In the 3rd. Successful journeys; help from relations and neighbours. This position adds benevolence of mind, and kindness.

In the 4th. Unless much afflicted and ill-dignified, this shows success in life, especially towards the end, and the father in a good position with possessions. The native often acquires property; but evil aspects to Jupiter would indicate the contrary.

In the 5th. Model children, who will rise in the world. This position is good for gaming, sports and speculations, pleasure in life; if Jupiter is ill-aspected, the contrary.

In the 6th. Good health and faithful servants; benefits from the lower classes. If ill-aspected by the Sun, corrupted blood and deranged liver; in the common signs, trouble with the lungs; in the cardinal signs, deranged stomach and system.

In the 7th. A successful and happy marriage; favourable for partnerships and lawsuits; success as a lawyer. The native gets a good marriage partner; if afflicted, the reverse of all this.

In the 8th. Money by marriage and by will, unless badly afflicted.

In the 9th. A sincere, religious person, of high moral character. Fortunate long journeys, either by sea or land; success in science, art and publishing; should Jupiter be badly aspected, it would counteract all this.

In the 10th. Success in business; honour and esteem; a happy mother; success in life. Jupiter in this house, in good aspect to the luminaries, vouchsafes pence and prosperity; if in cross aspect, there would be little pence and prosperity.

In the 11th. Many faithful and valuable friends; realisation of hopes and desires; if in cross aspect, the reverse.

In the 12th. The native will have great power of attraction, and be successful in dealings with large cattle; but not so, if Jupiter is afflicted.

The Effect of Mars in each of the Twelve Houses.

In the 2nd. Great generosity; the native squanders his money and is lavish. May embarrass his fortune through rash actions in business and things speculative.

In the 3rd. Stubborn, perverse and headstrong; danger in travelling;

if afflicted, quarrels with and losses through brethren and neighbours, troubles through writings or short journeys.

In the 4th. Troubles with the home and the father. Bad for the eventide of life, if Mars be afflicted. In ♈ or ♑ and well-aspected, this planet vouchsafes some of this world's goods.

In the 5th. Trouble with offspring; if afflicting the luminaries, they will die early and suddenly either by accident or otherwise; fondness for gambling and speculation, causing great loss; very unfortunate in a lady's horoscope; often too fond of pleasure and dissipation. ♀ afflicted by ♂ in this house would cause the native to form a liaison.

In the 6th. Bad servants. In the common signs, liability to chest troubles; if ill-aspected by the Sun or Moon, liability to inflammatory distempers; in the fixed signs, bladder troubles, disease of the heart or throat; in the cardinal signs, headache, indigestion, acute rheumatism.

In the 7th. An unfavourable marriage; quarrels with the husband or wife, and if much afflicted, probable separation; ill-luck attends partnerships. It delays or prevents marriage in a female's horoscope. Begets many open enemies.

In the 8th. A lavish or wasteful marriage partner; quarrels through legacies, wills, and the marriage partner's pecuniary affairs.

In the 9th. Extremely obstinate and despotic, suspicious and critical to an intense degree, hostile to religion and creeds, sarcastic, perverse; a liar, if Mercury be afflicted, and most unamiable. Unfortunate long journeys, and if in a watery sign, danger of drowning; in the common signs and afflicting Mercury, hurt or malformation to feet or limbs.

In the 10th. Very conceited, pretentious, quick in anger and hasty in judgment, liable to much slander, an objectionable personality and aggressive; a man who aspires to martial honours and to rule others; a presumptuous man, pushful.

In the 11th. Bad and malicious friends; if afflicted, loss and injury through them.

In the 12th. Secret enemies; if afflicted, liability to false accusations and imprisonment; also assassination, if Mars afflicts the Sun or Moon. More than one royal personage has been assassinated who had Mars in the 12th and afflicting the luminaries.

The Effect of the Sun in each of the Twelve Houses.

In the 2nd. Great success in money matters, unless much afflicted; given to squandering and extravagance.

In the 3rd. If in watery or moveable signs, many short journeys; success and gain by writings, neighbours and municipal affairs; gives a resolute and stable character.

In the 4th. Fortunate for the father, unless afflicted; success at the evening of life; acquisition of property; if afflicted the reverse of all this.

In the 5th. Fond of company; gain by pleasure and speculation, if the sun be well-aspected. In the barren signs, this position denies offspring.

In the 6th. Bad health, if afflicted. In the fixed signs, all kinds of throat troubles, bladder affections, heart disease, weak back; in the common signs, liability to consumption and all kinds of chest disease, particularly if afflicted by Saturn or the Moon; in the cardinal signs, disordered system and stomach, head troubles.

In the 7th. Good for partnerships, honour, distinction, and business; opposition from powerful persons; a probable public position; a good marriage partner, independent in character.

In the 8th. Wasteful or lavish, husband or wife; rich partner in marriage, gain by will or legacy if well-aspected.

In the 9th. In mind firm, noble, constant, and just; of a sincere and devout character. In watery signs, successful long journeys by sea; fortunate in publishing; evilly aspected, there is little gain.

In the 10th. Success in business; honours; acquisition of money and good fortune comes to the mother, when well-aspected.

In the 11th. Faithful and powerful friends, from whom the native will benefit. If afflicted, loss by friends.

In the 12th. If afflicted, powerful secret enemies.

The Effect of Venus in each of the Twelve Houses.

In the 2nd. Some prosperity, if well-aspected; if afflicted by Mars or Jupiter, the native will be extravagant.

In the 3rd. Gives imagination, popularity, love of mirth and witticism; successful short journeys; if aspected by Mercury, poetical, musical, and literary talent; a fun-loving spirit prevails.

In the 4th. Success in the closing years of life, during which the native will be occupied by literature, art, or music; help from the father, who will be prosperous; if afflicted, the native is not prosperous.

In the 5th. Successful speculations; fond of all kinds of pleasures, amusements, and much given to the society of the other sex; loving, dutiful offspring.

In the 6th. Gain by servants or employees.

In the 7th. Success and happiness in marriage; fortunate in business, partnerships, and law; if Venus is afflicted all this is overthrown.

In the 8th. Gain by marriage and legacies, unless afflicted.

In the 9th. Successful and pleasant journeys; the native will have great veneration for all things Divine; will be mirthful, poetic, conscientious, with artistic and musical ability; if aspected by Mars and Mercury, a keen sense of the ludicrous; well-aspected by Mercury, beauty of thought, keen appreciation of the beautiful and a vivid imagination.

In the 10th. A successful life, honour, love of pleasure and fortunate therein; good fortune to the mother when well-aspected. This position often brings fame or auspicious notoriety.

In the 11*th.* Many friends, by whom the native gains, for they contribute to his happiness; realisation of hopes and wishes; not so, if Venus is afflicted.

In the 12*th.* Probable success in dealing in large cattle; if much afflicted, plotters and schemers will make trouble.

THE EFFECT OF MERCURY IN EACH OF THE TWELVE HOUSES.

In the 2*nd.* If well-aspected, a modicum of success in literature and money matters.

In the 3*rd.* Cultured, fond of scientific studies, clever; in the fixed signs, concentration of thought; in the moveable signs, apt to see both sides of a question, but unable to do himself justice through lack of tenacity of purpose. The native is too versatile, with too rapid sequence of ideas.

In the 4*th.* If well-aspected, success as an estate agent, printer, engineer.

In the 5*th.* In barren signs, denies children; if afflicted in other signs, they may have some infirmity.

In the 6*th.* Troubles from servants, if afflicted. In the common signs, trouble with the respiratory organs; if much afflicted in ♐, ♓ or ♍, mental disease is to be feared.

In the 7*th.* Rather clever wife or husband; if afflicted, quarrels with wife or husband; if well-aspected, the native might acquire a public post connected with science or literature.

In the 8*th.* Legacies and money by marriage if well-aspected: not otherwise.

In the 9*th.* Good mental abilities; intuitive, intellectual, scientific; the latter especially if in scientific signs; success in publishing and writing, but if ill-aspected there is little ability and little gain.

In the 10*th.* Literary ability; a teacher or schoolmaster. Intuitive and practical in judgment. Much depends on the sign Mercury occupies; if afflicted the abilities are poor.

In the 11*th.* Help from friends, unless this planet is afflicted.

In the 12*th.* If afflicted, many secret enemies.

THE EFFECT OF THE MOON IN EACH OF THE HOUSES.

In the 2*nd.* Pence and prosperity if well-aspected; if afflicted by Saturn, without the support of Jupiter or Venus, the native will be poor.

In the 3*rd.* Many successful short journeys; help from brethren and neighbours; a studious mind, unless afflicted.

In the 4*th.* Many changes; if well-dignified and aspected, a successful farmer or builder. A competence is acquired.

In the 5th. Certainty of children, and in ♋ or ♓ a very large family; afflicted by Saturn, with no good aspect from Jupiter or Venus, much sickness among them; success in speculation and in connection with places of amusement when well aspected.

In the 6th. If afflicted, ill-health. In common signs, liability to consumption and lung disease; in the fixed signs, trouble with the throat, bladder and organic weakness of the heart; in the cardinal signs, derangement of the stomach and often headaches. Afflicted by Mars, inflammatory attacks and kidney disease; by Jupiter, the liver, blood and stomach are affected; by Mercury, liability to brain disease.

In the 7th. If unafflicted, a happy marriage; fortunate partnership; success in public dealing. The Moon is best free from the influence of Uranus. Bad aspects of Saturn, Uranus or Mars to the Moon would cause infelicity and separation.

In the 8th. If unafflicted, money by marriage, gain by legacies, especially if befriended by Venus or Jupiter. If much afflicted by Mars, Saturn or Uranus, danger of serious accidents and a violent death; no money by marriage.

In the 9th. Long journeys and voyages; a studious mind. Aspected by Uranus, love of the occult, bigoted in religion and apt to change creed; aspected by Mercury, a quick comprehensive mind.

In the 10th. If well-aspected, great success in life and in business as a merchant; if afflicted, little remunerative business; success to the mother; help from friends. Changes of avocation, if the Moon be in moveable signs.

In the 11th. If well-dignified and aspected, great assistance from friends; if afflicted, loss by friends.

In the 12th. If afflicted, many secret foes

CHAPTER VIII.

THE EFFECTS OF THE CONJUNCTION OF SIGNIFICATORS.

The lord of the ascendant, or planets in the ascendant or 1st house are significators of the native.

Example:—If ♈ ascend, ♂ is significator or lord of the ascendant; if ♉ or ♎, ♀ is significator; if ♐ or ♓, ♃ is significator; and if ♑, ♄ is significator; ♋ the ☽; ♊ or ♍, ☿; ♌ the ☉.

The ☌ of ♄ and ♃ and ♄ significator, *i.e.*, lord of the ascendant, or posited in the ascendant or 1st house, though not actually in the ascendant, vouchsafes possessions, inheritance and gain from the product of the land; for Jupiter rules the fruits of the earth. The disposition is grave, sober, honest and laborious, if ♃ is well-dignified; if he is not well-dignified, *i.e.*, posited in ♍, the native is vain, obstinate, and not so fortunate. *If ♃ be significator and ♄ be dignified*, the native will lack courage, being suspicious, grave, austere, unsociable, acquisitive, and covetous; he will acquire much money. *If ♄ be ill-dignified*, the native is ignoble, dull, shy, cunning, with hypocrisy and selfishness, therefore, less fortunate.

The ☌ of ♄ and ♂. *If ♄ be significator and ♂ well-dignified*, the native is rash, unruly, quarrelsome, obdurate, severe, and often cruel; he may gain preferment in warlike capacities, but, by cruel and unworthy conduct, may merit and find disgrace. *If ♂ be ill-dignified*, the native will be treacherous, malignant, and actively hostile. *If ♂ be significator and ♄ well-dignified*, the native will be less courageous, yet seemingly rash and daring, cruel, rarely forgiving; his career will be chequered, and he will over-reach others. *If ♄ be ill-dignified*, the native will be malicious, cowardly, wicked, deceitful and hypocritical.

The ☌ of ♄ and the ☉. *If ♄ be significator*, the native is proud, lofty, not fortunate, and often experiences mortification from his superiors; this conjunction often signifies a mean, servile, disagreeable condition and oppression;

the native is ignoble and unhappy. *If the ☉ be ill-dignified*, the fortunes are worse. *If the ☉ be significator and ♄ be well-dignified*, the native is proud, mean, deceitful, careless, and may lose his or her inheritance, or break his limbs by accidents. *If ♄ be ill-dignified*, his condition is base and his fortunes bad ; a mixture of pride, meanness, and covetousness.

The ☌ of ♄ and ♀. *If Saturn be significator and well-dignified*, the native is sensual, licentious, much attached to women, by whom he gains, and his disposition, though grave, mild and quiet, is addicted to pleasure ; he is tolerably fortunate. *If Venus be ill-dignified*, he is mean, effeminate, selfish, deceitful, and plunges into dissipation ; he may even marry a woman of indifferent character, where he would find misery. *If ♀ be significator and ♄ well-dignified*, the native will lack courage, though he will be wise, careful of his own affairs, but not very fortunate in his undertakings, in spite of prudence and caution ; moderate in his desires, grave, steady, austere, and of few words. *If ♄ be ill-dignified*, he is sensuous, malignant, cruel, stubborn, envious, possessing dissimulation.

The ☌ of ♄ and ☿. *If ♄ be significator*, the native is subtle, crafty, though possessing good judgment, inclined to research, often learned, a person of much gravity, not of amiable manners ; he may be supercilious and pedantic ; a man of policy, covetous and proud, with some elocutionary power. *If ☿ be significator*, there is an impediment in the speech, the native is dull, suspicious, mean, cowardly, covetous, weak-minded (if ☿ be ill-dignified), conceited, indolent, talkative, ignorant. ☿ in bad aspect to the ☽ makes the person dishonest, artful, treacherous, base and unfortunate. *If ☿ be significator and ♄ well-dignified*, the native is fearful, reserved, and slow in action or movement ; cool, secretive, cautious, and calculating ; his close-fistedness frequently enables him to scrape a fortune together ; he schemes to some purpose, which he turns to good account ; he is selfish and unsociable. *If ♄ be ill-dignified*, the native is treacherous, malignant, envious of the abilities of others, of shallow judgment, mistrustful, dishonest, deeply revengeful, obstinate, intractable, and stupid.

The ☌ of ♄ and the ☽. This indicates a poor and obscure person. *If ♄ be significator*, there is a mutable spirit, which impels the native to do things and then repent of them ; he is restless and unsettled in his purposes, and unfortunate. *When the ☽ is well-dignified*, the native is acute and of sound judgment, provided ☿ is free from affliction ; but changes will bring reverses of fortune, from which he may derive benefits in the end. *If the ☽ be ill-dignified*, it denotes great misfortunes and losses, beggary by the native's own folly, instability, obscurity, the mean and the wretched. An evil aspect of ♂ to the ☽ may bring the native to an untimely end. *If the ☽ be significator*, the native is poor, miserable, dejected, of unpleasant manners, sullen disposition, unfortunate, covetous, suspicious, cautious ; he frequently commits the most unaccountable errors in affairs of the greatest importance ; the mind is uncertain, the native lacks decision. *If the ☽ be significator and ♄ well-dignified*, the native will be timid, suspicious, austere, morose, reserved, covetous, slow, of good judgment, laborious, not very aspiring or nice in manners, he makes money by his own exertions. *If ♄ be ill-dignified*, the native is cruel, malicious, possessing secret vindictiveness; avaricious, changeable, and often wasting his means without end or design; generally this person is hated, avoided, and unfortunate.

N.B.—The student should observe that the conjunction operates, as stated, when the significators are free from aspects of other planets; for a good aspect of ♀ or ♃ would mitigate the evil effects; whilst an aspect of ♂ would counteract the timidity and add boldness. But if the aspect of ♂ be a □ or ☍ it renders the native more cruel, ferocious, and prone to wickedness. A good aspect from the ☉ improves the native's character and fortune.

The ☌ of ♃ and ♂. ♃ *significator and Mars well-dignified*, the native is bold, hasty, soon angry, proud, magnanimous, greatly-daring, often presumptuous and enterprising; a warlike character. *If Mars be ill-dignified*, the person is intolerant, unprincipled, strifeful, often susceptible to dissipation. ♂ *significator and* ♃ *well-dignified*, the native is pious, just, noble; a man of piety, who often rises high in the church. ♃ *ill-dignified*, he is more ignoble; not so good a man.

The ☌ of ♃ and the ☉. ♃ *significator*, brings much good fortune to the person.

The ☌ of ♃ and ♀. ♀ *significator*, the native will be very attractive, handsome; very happy in nature, and fortunate; virtuous, pious. ♃ *significator*, the person is rich and prosperous, with many fine qualities.

The ☌ of ♃ and ☿. ♃ *significator and well-dignified*, the native is virtuous, wise, pious; a scholar, eloquent, a man of great capacity for learning; sometimes he becomes a divine. *If ☿ is ill-dignified*, the person is less clever, but will be serious and grave. ☿ *significator and* ♃ *well-dignified*, the native is mild, gentle, amiable; a man of abilities and sympathy; he is less clever, if ♃ is ill-dignified.

The ☌ of ♃ and ☽. ♃ *significator*, the native is mutable in mind; a traveller; often restless, good-natured; he is singularly fortunate and prosperous. ♃ *ill-dignified*, he will be good-natured but even less stable; though still successful. ☽ *significator and* ♃ *well-dignified*, the native is noble, magnanimous; he acquires honours, and is high in the esteem of others.

The ☌ of ♂ and ☉. ♂ *significator*, the native is proud, arrogant, with a daring, boasting, and impulsive spirit; his life is often cut short by accidents or feverish distempers; he may acquire martial honours and money by strife and violence. ☉ *significator and* ♂ *well-dignified*, the native is brave as a Nelson, but headstrong, violent and rash; he may end his days on the battlefield, or by a fever. ♂ *ill-dignified*, the native is even more rash and cruel; he may commit murder or violence in his rash moods.

♂ ☌ ♀ and ♂ significator, the native is hasty-tempered, but good-natured, and readily forgives; he is susceptible to feminine influence, amorous, gentle, kind, courteous. ♀ *ill-dignified*, the person may form dishonourable

connections, to his detriment; may become prodigal, dissipated. ♀ *significator and ♂ well-dignified*, the native will be proud, quarrelsome, amorous to a large degree, though brave, hasty, rash, rowdy. ♂ *ill-dignified*, the person is cruel, vindictive, following wickedness and debauchery.

♂ ☌ ☿. ♂ *significator and ☿ well-dignified*, the native has much acuteness, sharpness of wit, a smatterer in learning, pragmatical; often swayed by passion; such people have presence of mind, ready wit, much imagination, a quick penetration; often possessing mathematical skill. ☿ *ill-dignified*, the person is ill-disposed, a great babbler; often slippery or knavish and disloyal. ☿ *significator and ♂ well-dignified*, the native has courage, presence of mind, ready wit. ♂ *ill-dignified*, the person is treacherous and will work much mischief; may commit a felony; such people may be thieves or robbers, and impostors.

♂ ☌ ☽. ♂ *significator and ☽ well-dignified*, the native is changeable, though bold, enterprising, evil-tempered; may be a wandering adventurer. ☽ *ill-dignified*, a vulgar, base, mean person, changeable, foolish; he may be given to drink and follow evil courses. ☽ *significator and ♂ well-dignified*, the native is rash, unruly, of poor intelligence, though courageous, enterprising, quarrelsome; he may be a thief or an assassin. ♂ *ill-dignified*, the person is violent, furious, malignant, treacherous, cruel; he may be a murderer, a robber, or a traitor.

☉ ☌ ♀. ☉ *significator and ♀ well-dignified*, makes the native magnanimous, ambitious; he excels at social functions, loves to perform great actions; he would do much for honour and more for glory; such a person would be extravagant. ♀ *significator*, the native will be proud, prodigal. But if the ☉ *be ill-dignified*, the person is mean; the native meets with crosses, vexations, and is sometimes unhealthy.

☉ ⚺ ☿ *and* ☉ ☌ ☿. ☉ *significator and ☿ well-dignified*, the native has wit, ingenuity, and acquires learning; there is aptitude for languages, the study of science, business aptitude, and a practical judgment. ☿ *significator*, the abilities are much the same; he is a man of policy. ☉ *well-dignified*, the person is more successful in business.

☉ ☌ ☽. ☉ *significator and ☽ well-dignified*, brings gain by travelling; a man of spirit, who aims high; often changeable and restless; therefore, such a person performs little through incontinuity; the fortunes are unstable. ☽ *ill-dignified*, the native will be unsteady, less healthy. ☽ *significator*, the eyesight may suffer; the native will be proud, aspiring to perform noble actions; but he will often fall short of that to which he aspires; he is unstable and lacks resolution.

♀ ☌ ☿. ♀ *significator and ☿ well-dignified*, makes the native handsome, ingenious, witty, eloquent, courteous; often a musician, artist; or possessing literary ability; it begets aptitude for learning, adding wisdom; an excellent disposition. ☿ *ill-dignified*, the abilities and disposition are not so good. ☿ *significator and ♀ well-dignified*, the native has elegance, beauty, wisdom, goodness of heart, tenderness, delicacy of temperament, compassion and modesty; and, indeed, all those nice qualities which make life go smoothly; the native may have oratorical gifts. ♀ *ill-dignified*, the native, though handsome, will be susceptible to over-indulgence in the pleasures of Venus, to his detriment and loss.

♀ ☌ ☽. ♀ *significator and* ☽ *well-dignified*, a good-natured, easy-tempered, mutable, unstable, but fortunate person; possessing dignity, self-importance, pride. ☽ *ill-dignified*, the person will be foolish as well as unstable; loquacious, with a vaunting spirit. ☽ *significator and* ♀ *well-dignified*, the native is of pleasing manners; he may attain proficiency in arts; such people are fond of company, and command the admiration of others. ♀ *ill-dignified*, the native is too much given to pleasure; foolish and careless.

☿ ☌ ☽. ☿ *significator and* ☽ *well-dignified*, adds wit, a good understanding, much intuition; such people are fond of travelling, changeable, unsteady. ☽ *significator and* ☿ *well-dignified*, the abilities are equally good; the native may be clever in mathematics, arts, sciences; he delights in journeys, and is mutable in mind. ☿ *ill-dignified*, there is less ability; less capacity for knowledge.

THE EFFECTS OF THE SEXTILES, SEMI-SEXTILES, SEMI-QUINTILES, QUINTILES, SEPTILES,* BIQUINTILES, AND TRINES OF SIGNIFICATORS.

The ✶, ⚺, Sq, Q, Bq, △ *of* ♄ *and* ♃. ♄ *significator*, the native is wise, grave, discreet, pious, sober; he sometimes acquires church preferment and wealth by agriculture; the native gains by will or inheritances. ♃ *significator*, the native is sad or melancholy, reserved, fearful, cautious, persevering.

The ✶, ⚺, Sq, Q, Bq, △ *of* ♄ *and* ♂. ♄ *significator*, the native has, in addition to his wariness and caution, some boldness and courage, which overcome the timidity; he is generous, though easily irritated and angry; active, enterprising, confident, and resentful. ♂ *significator*, the native is cautious, deliberate, pertinacious. resolute, prudent, with the martial spirit at the bottom; he has the iron hand.

The ✶, ⚺, Sq, Q, Bq, △ *of* ♄ *and* ☉. ♄ *significator*, the native is austere, passionate, apparently generous and noble, vindictive. ☉ *significator*, he is covetous, fearful, mean, vaunting in spirit, conceited, obstinate. ♄ *ill-dignified*, makes the person malicious, and extravagance may replace meanness.

The ✶, ⚺, Sq, Q, Bq, △ *of* ♄ *and* ♀. ♄ *significator*, the native is

* A new aspect of 52°. See also 105° and Semi-demi quintile of 18°.

pleasure-loving, extravagant, susceptible to feminine influence and voluptuousness. ♀ *significator*, the native is affable, quiet, modest, reserved, artful, grave, retiring, and not inclined to marriage.

The ⚹, ⊻, Sq, Q, Bq, △ *of* ♄ *and* ☿. ♄ *significator*, the native is ingenious, studious, subtle, reserved; he has more conceit than ability; he is artful, grave, inquisitive; a man of whims. ☿ *significator*, the native is peevish, discontented, dejected, fanciful, studious, subtle, reserved, mean, inventive; such people generally study arts and sciences; but if ♄ be ill-dignified, the person accomplishes little.

The ⚹, ⊻, Sq, Q, Bq, △ *of* ♄ *and* ☽. ♄ *significator*, the native is changeable, fearful, wilful, jealous, mistrustful. ☽ *significator*, the native is coldly reserved, mean in his actions, vain, conceited, yet deliberate, wilful; he acts meanly, with cold deliberation.

The ⚹, ⊻, Sq, Q, Bq, △ *of* ♃ *and* ♂. ♃ *significator*, a bold, noble, free, generous, ambitious, honourable person, desirous to rule, resolute, and subtle; he is fortunate in war, clever in chemistry, or skilful in surgery. If ♂ is weak, the native is not so fortunate. ♂ *significator*, the native is cheerful, merry, jovial, high-minded, honourable, enterprising, just, courageous, and pious; a man of valour, and of many virtues.

☉ 36° ♀ *and* ☉ ⊻ ♀. ♀ *significator*, begets a love of music, the drama, singing. ☉ *significator*, love of social distinction, public affairs and municipal work.

The ⚹ ⊻, Sq, Q, Bq, △ *of* ♃ *and* ☉. ♃ *significator*, prefigures a lofty, courageous, noble, generous, magnanimous, and fortunate person; but even more fortunate if the Sun be strong; if the Sun be weak, the person is moderately fortunate. ☉ *significator*, the native is high-minded, noble, just, generous, honourable, a man of great spirit, he loves to perform beneficent and honourable acts.

The ⚹, ⊻, Sq, Q, Bq, △ *of* ♃ *and* ♀. ♃ *significator*, the native is handsome, loving, kindly, pleasant, courteous, exceedingly good-natured, generally fortunate, and often wealthy; such people rise in life and acquire titular honours. ♀ *ill-dignified*, there may be too much fondness for pleasure and imprudence; honours may not be attained. ♀ *significator*, a comely, honourable, virtuous, noble, just and generous person, possessing piety. ♃ *ill-dignified*, there is less nobility of character.

The ⚹, ⊻, Sq, Q, Bq, △ *of* ♃ *and* ☿. ♃ *significator*, indicates a good, virtuous, just, ingenious person, of subtle wit, eloquence, sound judgment, good reasoning powers; he acquires learning, is affable, courteous, mild, free-spirited, perfectly trusty; the mind is receptive for learning. ♃ *ill-dignified*, the endowments and fortune are to some degree diminished. ☿ *significator*, all the good abilities and good fortune are vouchsafed to the native. ☿ *ill-dignified*, the native's good fortune and abilities are impaired.

The ⚹ ⊻, Sq, Q, Bq, △ *of* ♃ *and* ☽. ♃ *significator*, a good, just, virtuous man, of many fine qualities; he may become a great traveller; loquacious, a man of self-esteem, he is generally a great favourite with women. ☽ *ill-dignified,* the native is less fortunate. ☽ *significator,* a just, charitable, sincere person; noble, aspiring to honourable things.

The ✱, ⊻, Sq, Q, Bq, △ *of* ♂ *and* ☉. ♂ *significator,* the native rises, often becomes great or eminent; he has the favour of those in power. It is said to be the aspect of honour and action; the native rises rapidly in the army or navy. He is witty, ingenious, trusty, faithful, courteous and friendly. Such people inspire confidence in others. ☉ *significator,* a man of valour, often victorious in life's battle; high-spirited, courageous, he may attain military honours. A man of vigour, strong in limb and character; he believes in himself and his own invincible talents. Impelled on by great ambition, great and magnanimous, a true friend; he invariably rises above his sphere of birth. If, however, ♂ *be ill-dignified,* the native is less noble and less successful. The ☉ *ill-dignified,* the fortunes will not be so good, and the qualities will be less noble.

The ✱, ⊻, Sq, Q, Bq, △ *of* ♂ *and* ♀. ♂ *significator,* the native seeks pleasure, female society, and has many love-affairs. He is highly susceptible to feminine influence; loves women, pleasure, gaming, and is extravagant, improvident, ill-natured, or nice and courteous if with the other sex. ♀ *ill-dignified,* the character is more wild and loose. ♀ *strongly posited,* the native will be more tractable, generously-disposed, very prepossessing, vivacious, and more fortunate. ♂ *dignified,* the native is witty, ingenious. ♀ *significator,* the person is proud, vain, though bold, rash, artful; easily swayed by passion to anger, rashness, and hazardous adventures. ♀ *and* ♂ *ill-dignified,* the native will be voluptuous and unprincipled.

The ✱, ⊻, Sq, Q, Bq, △ *of* ♂ *and* ☿. ♂ *significator,* this gives good abilities, making the person ingenious, eloquent, confident, prudent, bold, subtle, acute in mind, penetrating, studious, fond of arts or sciences, sometimes hasty, swayed by passion, and crafty. ☿ *ill-dignified,* the native is superficial in mind, more crafty, with a vaunting and unprincipled spirit. ☿ *significator,* the native is courageous, ingenious, often a mathematician; a man of ready wit, acuteness; with much self-esteem, subtlety and great confidence. ♂ *ill-dignified,* the person is conceited, often rash, fond of gaming, following wild courses.

The ✱, ⊻, Sq, Q, Bq, △ *of* ♂ *and* ☽. ♂ *significator,* a loquacious, mutable, restless, subtle person. Such people travel much and gain thereby; often furious and rash, but soon appeased. ☽ *well-dignified,* the native is fairly fortunate. But ☽ *ill-dignified,* he gains little by journeys and his fortunes are less propitious. ♂ *strongly posited,* the native has fascinating powers over women. If ♂ is weak the native is more servile, less fortunate. ☽ *significator,* a high-spirited, passionate, ambitious person; very mutable in mind and consequently of unstable fortunes.

The ✱, ⊻, Sq, Q, Bq, △ *of* ☉ *and* ☽. ☉ *significator,* the native is fortunate, often eminent; the favourite of the multitude, for he often acquires money and honours. He is sure to have many followers or admirers; he is pleasant, cheerful, good-natured, kind-hearted, fond of travelling. The ☽ *ill-aspected* or ill-dignified, the native's fortune is impaired. ☽ *significator*, the native is proud, ambitious, generally successful. He will do much for honour and glory, both of which he often attains, unless the ☽ *be weakly posited.* He is mutable in mind.

The ✱, ⊻, Sq, ♀ *and* ☿. ♀ *significator*, a witty, ingenious, good-natured person; possessing finesse, the gift of oratory; aptitude for arts, sciences, or music; a learned and polite man. ☿ *significator*, a courteous, amorous, wise, prudent, just person; fond of learning, gentle, kindly, pleasing, elegant. ♀ *ill-dignified*, the native is less accomplished, the mind less pure. The native is addicted to loose desires and prodigality. ☿ *ill-dignified*, there is more of the vicious than the virtuous; more folly than wisdom.

The ✱, ⊻, Sq, Q, Bq, △ *of* ♀ *and* ☽. ♀ *significator*, honours, the favour of influential women; he may become the favourite of the multitude. He is versatile even unto mutability; though prepossessing, engaging, he accomplishes little through an inconstant mind. ☽ *well-dignified*, the fortune is good though the mind is unstable. ☽ *significator*, an amorous, gentle, obliging, conscientious person. ☽ *or* ♀ *ill-dignified*, the native succumbs to vice and is unfortunate.

The ✱, ⊻, Sq, Q, Bq, △ *of* ☽ *and* ☿. ☿ *significator*, a witty, ingenious person, of good abilities, and quick penetration, mutable in mind, lacking resolution; diplomatic, dissimulative, though pleasant; the native is sometimes reserved, with a little melancholy. *The* ☽ *ill-dignified*, makes the person insincere. ☽ *significator*, a more subtle and crafty person, with self-love, reserve and sadness; clever in arts or sciences; may be a good orator or a good advocate. ☽ *ill-dignified*, the native is less fortunate, less reliable and more receptive; he has more artifice and is more shifty.

N.B.—We have found that the evil aspects of Uranus to the Sun have an adverse influence upon the native's fortune through life, even should the Sun have the good aspects of Mars and Jupiter. This is supported by the horoscope of Wagner the composer.

The good aspects of Uranus to the Sun, coinciding with good aspects of Jupiter and Mars to the Sun, make the native singularly fortunate. This is supported by the horoscopes of Emerson, Prince Bismarck; we are aware, of course, that Venus was on the mid-heaven in the horoscope of the latter.

Berlioz had ☉ ✱ ♅; ☉ ☌ ♂; but he was fortunate.

Mozart was unsuccessful pecuniarily, and the ☽ was afflicted by ♅.

Chopin had ☉ △ ♅, though the Sun was afflicted by ♂ and ♄; he met with pence and prosperity, though he was unfortunate in love and suffered in health.

We can instance the case of a lady who had ☉ rising □ ♅, though △ ♂ and ✱ ♃; she was most unfortunate pecuniarily.

The aspects of ☽ to ♅, when either are significators, incline to changes and unsettledness.

The good aspects of ☿ and ♅ incline to study, occultism, and originality.

The good aspects of Neptune bring much good fortune, as in the case of Verdi, though the Sun was afflicted by Saturn. The ☌ was in △ to ♃, ☿ △ ♂, ☿ ⚹ ♆ and ☉ ⚹ ♆.

Mozart was unfortunate, and the Sun was opposed to Neptune, though the Sun was also conjoined with Saturn. He was often in poverty and had a pauper's grave, though ♃ was in the 2nd house, ⚹ ☽. But he made much money.

Chopin was unfortunate in love affairs, though Jupiter was on the western angle; but the ☉ was in that angle, □ ♆ and □ ♄, and the Moon was in square to Neptune and ♄, and in △ with ♀.

THE EFFECTS OF SQUARES, SEMI-SQUARES, SESQUI-QUADRATES, AND OPPOSITIONS OF SIGNIFICATORS.

The □, ∠, ⚼ and ☍ of ♄ and ♃. ♄ *significator*, the native meets with many troubles, some persecution; he clashes with creedists and experiences much vexation; in character he is ignoble and selfish; often guilty of folly. ♃ *significator*, the native has a troubled course of life, is low-spirited, cross, peevish and unhappy; he meets with crosses; others treat him with contempt; he is generally unfortunate.

The □, ∠, ⚼ and ☍ of ♄ and ♂. ♄ *significator*, the person is cruel, malicious, treacherous, proud, soon angry, ungrateful and wicked. Indeed, the worst dispositions are produced when Saturn or Mars occupies the ascendant, and are found in □ or ☍ to each other, especially if either of these planets afflicts the Moon or Mercury. ♂ *significator*, the native is just as malicious, treacherous, rebellious and wilful, but more turbulent; he is often melancholy and commits suicide; he does not escape accidents, injuries or wounds; his peculiarity is a revengeful nature; he never forgives.

The □, ∠, ⚼ and ☍ of ♄ and ☉. ♄ *significator*, makes the native proud, prodigal, ambitious, apparently revengeful; but the boldness and courage are more apparent than real; he can be overbearing and disagreeable in manners. ☉ *significator*, the native is just as spiteful, malicious and false; he will vaunt and is proud, impudent, obstinate and revengeful; but his fearful and timorous temperament restrains him; his end and his life are generally unhappy ones.

The □, ∠, ⚼ and ☍ of ♄ and ♀. ♄ *significator*, this begets voluptuousness, vice, infamy, dissipation; the person is too susceptible to the pleasures of Venus, is prodigal in his expenses. ♀ *significator*, makes the person sly, artful, addicted to dissipation, base, deceitful and unfortunate; a man of nervous fears and some reserve.

The □, ∠, ⚼ and ☍ of ♄ and ☿. ♄ *significator*, a knave; cunning, treacherous, malicious, dull, stupid and sly. Bent upon mischief; untruthful and untrustworthy. ☿ *significator*, makes the native artful, contentious; he will vilify others. He is cowardly, often dejected, spitefully slanderous, often secretively thievish, perverse, self-willed, peculiarly envious. For he stirs up strife among his neighbours.

The □, ∠, ⚼ *and* ☍ *of* ♄ *and* ☽. ♄ *significator*; often a wanderer; unsettled, changeable, fretful, discontented and base. ☽ *significator*, the native is mean, cowardly, unhappy, dejected, jealous, suspicious, mistrustful, malicious, artful, melancholy.

The □, ⚼, ∠ *and* ☍ *of* ♃ *and* ♂. ♃ *significator*; a furious, rash, adventuresome, quarrelsome, subtle, resolute person; ambitious, ill-natured. A man of violent impulses, which sway him to his detriment. ♂ *significator*. Begets pride, ingratitude, insolence, atheism, daring, obstinacy, audacity and scorn. A haughty nature.

The □, ∠, ⚼ *and* ☍ *of* ♃ *and* ☉. ♃ *significator*, a vain, arrogant, prodigal person; with much love of approbation, and a desire to become distinguished, which is rarely gratified. He is wasteful with his substance; his lofty and noble appearance is unreal. ☉ *significator*, a proud, dissipated, wasteful, scornful, arrogant person.

The □, ∠, ⚼ *and* ☍ *of* ♃ *and* ♀. ♃ *significator*, extravagance, temptations to dissipation and intemperance. The disposition is not bad; but thoughtless and pleasure-loving. ♀ *significator*, the native lacks prudence; he is proud, prodigal, indulgent, pleasure-loving. He wastes his substance.

The □, ∠, ⚼ *and* ☍ *of* ♃ *and* ☿. ♃ *significator*; trouble, contention, perplexities, vexations; the native is unstable, foolish. He gets wrong impressions and is humorsome. ☿ *significator*; strife, conflicts, imprudence, folly, vexations. The native is unstable, a man of imagination and false impressions.

The □, ∠, ⚼ *and* ☍ *of* ♃ *and* ☽. ♃ *significator*; the native is foolish, loquacious, changeable, irresolute, indiscreet. ☽ *significator*; the native is proud, obstinate, comes into conflict with others, meets with crosses and losses through others.

The □, ∠, ⚼ *and* ☍ *of* ♂ *and* ☉. ♂ *significator*; the native is furious, proud, impulsively rash, violent, ambitious, brave; a hero on the battlefield. ☉ *significator*, a rash, daring, noisy, aggressive person; fevers or accidents sometimes cut short his days; his straits are often desperate, and he is prodigal.

The □, ∠, ⚼ *and* ☍ *of* ♂ *and* ♀. ♂ *significator*, a treacherous, malicious, prodigal, voluptuous person; he often follows gaming, drinking, is ill-natured; a boasting, ostentatious person. ♀ *significator*, a treacherous, mischievous, base, inconstant, wicked and voluptuous person; contentious, impertinent and quarrelsome.

The □, ∠, ⚼ *and* ☍ *of* ♂ *and* ☿. ♂ *significator*, a daringly wicked, artful, sharp, bold, impudent, treacherous, unsettled, conceited, humorsome person; easily offended; seldom pleased or of good humour. ☿ *significator*, the native is bold, furious, desperate, cruel, malicious and obdurate; a villain, guilty of crimes, contentious and mischievous; often an assassin, a child of infamy.

The □, ∠, ▫ and ☍ of ♂ and ☽. ♂ *significator*, a low, vulgar, unprincipled, bitter-tongued, abusive, stupid, servile person. Such people defame and traduce the characters of others; the most ignoble of men. ☽ *significator*, an abusive, malicious, treacherous, mutable, rash, passionate, proud, mischievous, cruel person; he may travel and meet with an early death through fevers and accidents.

The ∠ of ☉ and ♀. ☉ *significator*, disappointments and strife; the native is proud and confident. ♀ *significator*, a vain, vaunting, self-assertive person; often disappointed.

The □, ∠, ▫ and ☍ of ☉ and ☽. ☉ *significator*, the native is proud, vain, changeable, mean, unstable, often a deceiver. ☽ *significator*, the native is obstinate and ambitious, but he meets with losses, crosses, and is easily mortified; there is great pride, sometimes there is an infirmity in the sight and blindness ensues if the Moon be with the Pleiades on the western angle, in ♉ 29°.

The ∠ of ♀ and ☿. ♀ *significator*, the native has a love of music and singing. ☿ *significator*, the native is indulgent, easy-going, fond of music.

The □, ∠, ▫ and ☍ of ♀ and ☽. ♀ *significator*, a vulgar, contentious, changeable, unsettled, quarrelsome person; indolent, silly, ignorant and conceited. ☽ *significator*, a voluptuous, impertinent, bold, ignoble, often dissolute person.

The □, ∠, ▫ and ☍ of ☿ and ☽. ☿ *significator*, the person is sharp, intuitive, but shifty, unsettled foolish, idle, proud, ignorant, disagreeable, loquacious and arrogant. ☽ *significator*, a knavish, cunning, unstable person.

CHAPTER IX.

HOW TO CAST THE HOROSCOPE.

It is necessary to call the student's attention to the fact that the earth revolves west to east on its axis. This motion makes the planets rise in the east, pass the mid-heaven, and set in the west; therefore the signs carrying the planets travel the way of the hands of a clock, east to west, *viâ* the mid-heaven. Of course, each planet is travelling (when not retrograde) west to east *viâ* the mid-heaven, increasing its longitude each day. The Moon, for instance, by increasing her longitude from 12 to nearly 16° per day, rises later, in consequence, each day. Thus a planet rising passes into the 12th house, then the 11th, etc. But a planet would also increase its longitude, and would pass from the 11th into the 12th, and from the 12th into the 1st house.

Mr. Arthur Pearson, of *Pearson's Weekly*, was born at 11 a.m. (local time*), February 24th, 1866, at Wookey, near Wells, Somersetshire. The latitude is 51°25′ north, and the longitude is 2½° west of Greenwich. The student should buy an Ephemeris for the year for which a horoscope is required. This being for the year 1866, turn to the end of the book (where a page of the Ephemeris for February, 1866, has been inserted), and opposite February 24th you will find the sidereal time (which is the Sun's right ascension in hours, minutes and seconds); this sidereal time is 22h. 16m. 32sec. From this you must deduct 1h., because he was born at one hour before noon, this will leave 21h. 16m. 32sec.

(If, however, 11 a.m. is Greenwich time, and not true local time, the longitude must be multiplied by 4; thus Wookey, near Wells, Somerset, is 2½° west longitude from Greenwich, which multiplied by 4 = 10m. These 10m. must be deducted from 21h. 16m. 32sec., which leaves 21h. 6m. 32sec., therefore when it is 11 a.m. in London, it is 10.50 a.m. at Wookey, near Wells. Had his birthplace been in 2½° of east longitude, 10m. would have

* We have found that, many years ago, most churches regulated their clocks by a sun dial. But to-day they mostly keep Greenwich time.

to be added, that is to say, if the time used was Greenwich time; this time is now used by all our railways all through England.

It is not known by Mr. Pearson if the time given is local or Greenwich time, so the test horoscope, which appeared in *Borderland*, was computed for 11 a.m. (local time).

We now turn to the "Tables of Houses" (which are found at the end of each Ephemeris) for latitude 51°25' north; the nearest to this are London Tables. The student must now search among the columns marked "Sidereal Time" for the time nearest to 21h. 16m. 32sec.; he will find 21h. 17m. 50sec. to be the nearest.

At the top of the column next to the sidereal time the student will find 10♒. The number stands for the house, and the sign shows that it should be put on that house; so he would put ♒ on the cusp of the 10th house, and the number 17, which is immediately beside the sidereal time, and in this first column is the number of degrees; thus the student will have on the cusp of the 10th house ♒ 17°. The second column records 11♒, but if the student looks down the column he will find that ♓ has succeeded that sign before 21h. 17m. 50sec., and so ♓ 16° must be placed on the cusp of the 11th house. The third column records 12♈, 12th house, but ♉ 2° must be placed there. The fourth column records ascendant ♊, this means that the sign ♊ is the ascendant (or on the cusp of the 1st house), so ♊ 22°53' must be placed there. The fifth column records 2♊, but on looking lower down, the student will find that ♋ has succeeded ♊, and so ♋ 10° must be placed on the cusp of the 2nd house. The sixth column records 3♋, and so ♋ 27° must be placed on the cusp of the 3rd house.

The student will then proceed to find the opposite signs to those already given. The 17th degree of ♌ should be placed on the cusp of the 4th house (♌ being opposite ♒), the 16th degree of ♍ on the cusp of the 5th house (♍ being opposite ♓), the 2nd degree of ♏ on the cusp of the 6th house (♏ being opposite ♉), the 22nd degree and 53rd minute of ♐ is placed on the cusp of the 7th house (♐ being opposite ♊), ♑ is opposite ♋, and is, therefore, placed on the 8th and 9th houses.

Having put the proper sign on the cusp of each of the houses, the student must now see whether the twelve signs of the Zodiac are there (for sometimes two or more signs may be intercepted); those signs which have been omitted or intercepted will follow in natural sequence, as for instance: Aries follows Pisces, and, as it was intercepted in this horoscope, it must come directly after Pisces, and so is put in the middle of the 11th house. The same remark applies to Libra, which comes after Virgo, and should be placed in the middle of the 5th house. Had Mr. Pearson been born six hours before noon (*i.e.*, 6 a.m.), six hours would have to be deducted, and one minute also would be taken from the remainder, as the acceleration of sidereal time is at the rate of nearly four minutes per day. On the other hand, in a horoscope computed for 6 p.m., the six hours after noon would have to be added to the sidereal time, and a minute for the acceleration of sidereal time. It should also be understood that when the sum exceeds twenty-four hours, this number should be deducted. Example:—

	H.	M.	S.
Sidereal time, noon, February 24th, 1866, is	22	16	32
Add	6	0	0
	28	16	32
Add 1 minute for acceleration of sidereal time		1	0
	28	17	32
Subtract 24 (the circle) hours	24	0	0
	4	17	32

Now seek in the Tables of Houses, the nearest to 4h. 17m. 32sec.

CHAPTER X.

HOW TO PLACE THE PLANETS IN THE HOROSCOPE.

The transposition of the planets from the Ephemeris to the horoscope is a very simple process, and a page of Ephemeris for February, 1866, is given at the end of this book as an example.

The motion of Uranus, Saturn and Jupiter is so slow, that they have moved but a few seconds in an hour, and may be taken from the Ephemeris without addition or subtraction from their longitudes. The motion of Mars is 46m. per day; therefore, nearly 2m. should be deducted from his position at noon. The progress of Venus is 1°15' per day (which is a little over 3m. per hour); therefore, 3m. should be deducted from the longitude of Venus, thus: ♀ 5° ♓ 19'−3'=5° ♓ 16'. The motion of Mercury is 1°49' per day, which is 4m. 32sec. per hour; therefore 4m. 32sec. should be deducted from 1° ♓ 34'0" noon. Thus: ☿ 1° ♓ 34'0"−4'32"=1° ♓ 29'28".

There now remain the places of the Sun and Moon, which are still to be calculated. The motion of the Sun is 1°0'18" per day, as will be seen in the Ephemeris; this means about 2m. 30sec. per hour. Therefore, 2m. should be deducted from the Sun's place at noon; thus: ☉ 5°40' is the Sun's longitude. That is the Sun's place at 11 a.m.

Rule for Calculating the Moon's place by Logarithms.

The seconds are discarded in this calculation.

Subtract the Moon's place, February 23rd, at noon, thus 5° 13'
from its place at noon, February 24th   21° 30'

That is, therefore, the Moon's motion in twenty-four hours. 13° 43'

Log. of 13°43' = 2430
Log. of 1h.   = 1·3802

Total 1·6232

The student must now look for this number (or the one nearest to it) in the page of logarithms; this will be found at the end of all recent Ephemerides. In the column headed degrees and opposite minutes 34 will be found 1·6269; this means that the Moon has moved no degrees and 34m. in one hour. Therefore, 34m. must be deducted from the Moon's place at noon, February 24th. Thus: ☽ 5°♋13′ − 34′ = 4°39′ Moon's place at one hour before noon. Taking the time 11 a.m. as true local time,* we have the Moon's place 4°39′ ♋.

The following is, perhaps, a simpler method of finding the places of the Moon and Planets, and would not require logarithms. The Moon's motion is reduced to minutes, and therefore 13°43′ reduced to minutes = 823′; the 24h. = 1440′; 1h. = 60′. The problem, then, is very simple, and is thus calculated.

If a heavenly body moves 823m. in 1440m., how much will it move in 60m.?

Multiply 823m. by 60m. and divide by 1440m. This will give 34m. and $\frac{7}{24}$ of a minute; and these 34m. (as already explained) should be deducted from the Moon's place at noon, February 24th.

Take one more example:—

If the Moon moves 12° in 24h., how much will she move in 6h.?

$$12° \text{ reduced to minutes} = 720′$$
$$24\text{h.} \quad ,, \quad ,, \quad = 1440′$$
$$6\text{h.} \quad ,, \quad ,, \quad = 360′$$

Multiply 720m. by 360m. and divide the result by 1440m., this will give 180m. or 3h.

The places of all the planets can be worked in this manner, and this will obviate the use of logarithms.

N.B.—Ephemerides can be had from the author.

The Moon's nodes or Dragon's Head (☊) and Dragon's Tail (☋), Cauda, have a retrograde motion of a little over 3m. per day. ☊ 13°52′ ♎ is the north node, and the south node ☋ falls exactly opposite in 13°52′ ♈.

The aspects can be seen at a glance. Example: Venus is 5°16′ ♓, the Sun is in 5°40′ ♓, Mercury is in 1°29′ ♓; Mercury, Venus and the Sun, therefore, are in conjunction.

The Moon is in 4°39′ ♋, and is, therefore, in trine aspect to Mercury, Venus and the Sun; that is to say they are nearly 120° apart.

Uranus is also in trine to the Sun, Venus and Mercury, though this aspect is not so close. The Moon is in conjunction with Uranus, and in trine aspect to Saturn.

It will, of course, be understood, as previously explained, that a planet may be 6° or 9° short or over the 120°, and it is called a trine aspect, for it is within orb. The Moon, for instance, is but a degree short of 120° from the Sun and Venus, though she is 3° over the 120° from Mercury, whilst she is 8° short of the 120° from Saturn. The Sun is 7° short of 120° to Saturn and yet it is in trine aspect. A trine aspect would begin to be influential between the Sun and Jupiter when the distance was 109°, and would also be within orb at 129½°, whilst opposition aspects exceed 169° and 190° between the Sun and Moon and the planets.

* To-day, if Wookey near Wells is using Railway or Greenwich time, it is using a time which is 10 minutes faster than its own meridian time.

CHAPTER XI.

CHAPTER ON HEALTH.

In judging a horoscope, one naturally turns first to the length of life. It would seem useless to calculate the series of coming events if one were not destined to live to experience them.

We look to the luminaries, their relative strength, and the ascendant; for the malefics afflicting the Sun and Moon or ascendant cause sickness, hurts, and shorten life. But before beginning to study this chapter it is interesting to notice what the Chaldeans say:—

Those born with the Moon in the western angle, conjoined with the Pleiades (these stars are in 28° longitude of Taurus), are threatened with blindness, injuries or diseases to the eyes. John Milton, the blind poet, was born at 6 a.m., December 9th, 1608, when the Moon was exactly setting in conjunction with the Pleiades. The following *primâ facie* cases have vindicated the science under this head. A person born May 13th, 6 p.m., 1875, with the Sun and Mercury setting near the Pleiades, has very weak sight. Another person, born at noon, September 10th, 1865, has the Moon near the Pleiades, setting in the western angle, and his eyes are a continual source of trouble to him; he has once narrowly escaped blindness. The Sun with the Pleiades in any part of the heavens causes weak or short sight.

♈ rules the head and face.
♉ rules the neck and throat.
♊ rules the lungs, hands, arms, shoulders and nerves.
♋ rules the breast and stomach.
♌ rules the heart, back and spine.
♍ rules the bowels, belly and nerves.
♎ rules the reins and loins.
♏ rules the genital and urinary organs.
♐ rules the hips, thighs and nerves.
♑ rules the knees and ham-strings.
♒ rules the legs and ankles.
♓ rules the feet, toes and nerves.

The ailments which you are liable to contract horoscopically speaking, have nothing to do with those infirmities which come hereditarily. It must, therefore, be distinctly understood that the hereditary strength of constitution and vitality modify the weakness and deficiencies of the horoscopical impression, *i.e.*, the man or woman who inherits a vigorous body is less liable to the physical weakness imposed by the planets. When you know to what physical debility you are liable, then take steps to escape it. If you find indications of stomach trouble, then be careful as to diet, eat slowly, and masticate your food well, so as to give the weak stomach no occasion to rebel at indigestible and unwholesome foods.

The diseases are produced when the planets afflict the Sun or Moon; and the signs occupied by the afflicting planets and luminaries indicate the parts of the body which will suffer. The signs occupied by the afflicted Sun and Moon will also indicate the parts of the body which will become deranged, and especially will those parts of the body suffer which are ruled by the sign on the cusp of or intercepted in the 6th house if a Malefic be therein and afflicting either the Sun or Moon. The Sun or Moon in the 6th house afflicted by the Malefics causes ill-health and the sign occupied will indicate the infirmity. Saturn in the 6th house and afflicting the Sun is a sure cause of much ill-health. Thus Mars conjunction Sun causes fevers, inflammations and often dysentery. But of course Mars often causes accidents and sometimes operations.

The Sun afflicted by the Malefics when the Sun is found in Cancer invariably causes stomach or gastric troubles and liver disorders. When the Sun is afflicted by Saturn and Saturn is in Aquarius then he produces rheumatism, and if the Sun is in Taurus there will be throat trouble, influenza.

The diseases rarely occur until the subsequent adverse aspect is formed by the Promittor to the Sun or Moon; but in most cases (unless Saturn or the Sun occupy the 6th house) the person does not suffer till the Promittor afflicts the Sun in the Star Courses. All subsequent adverse aspects of the Promittors Mars, Saturn, Uranus and Neptune to the Sun, seriously assail the health or cause hurts, bodily pain. Mars, however, is the chief cause of violence to the person, hence the suffering is usually acute. Neptune in Pisces in Sesqui-quadrate to the Sun at the birth of a person caused gout and rheumatism when the Sun reached the quartile aspect to this Promittor at age 47.

Though the affliction of the Sun or Moon by Mars, Saturn, Uranus or Neptune in the horoscope causes diseases when the Sun again in the Star Courses forms an adverse aspect with the afflicting planet, it must not be forgotten that adverse aspects from the Malefics to the Sun (even when they are not unfriendly-disposed at birth) will often cause indisposition. In the case of an elderly person it may cause ill-health and in the case of an aged person even death. The aspects in the Star Courses of non-adverse Promittors have little power and rarely cause indisposition of a serious nature unless the person is physically weak, and unless the vitality and constitution are hereditarily very poor, serious ill-health may not be feared.

The affliction of the Moon by Saturn is not so detrimental to the health as the affliction of the Sun by that planet. Indeed, the adverse aspects of Saturn to the Sun are powerfully inimical to the health of both sexes, whilst adverse aspects of Saturn to the Moon in the horoscope of a woman do cause ill-health.

☽ OR ☉ ∠, □, ⊡, ☍ OR ☌ ♄, ♅, OR ♆ PROMITTORS.

Saturn, Uranus or Neptune in Aries.—Colds in the head, catarrh, stomach troubles, acidity, toothache, and a little deafness.

Saturn, Uranus or Neptune in Taurus.—Throat trouble and nervous depression.

Saturn, Uranus, Neptune in Gemini.—Inactive state of the system, lower vitality, digestive power more or less enfeebled, obstruction of the bile passages, and sometimes biliousness. The trouble is purely digestive and functional weakness, improperly digested food; hence jaundice, impure blood, and a tendency to consumption.

Saturn, Uranus or Neptune in Cancer.—Sometimes a weak stomach, not enough heat in the stomach; hence trouble with the digestive organs, poor blood and therefore tumours, scrofulous conditions, ulcerations, breast troubles, and a liability to contract ague.

Saturn, Uranus, Neptune in Leo.—Heart palpitation, pains in the back avoid over-exertion and excitement. Kidneys deranged. Be careful as to diet.

Saturn, Uranus or Neptune in Virgo.—Pains in the bowels, constipation, sometimes an impure state of the blood, depression and a disordered state of the system; consequently, often calculous concretion in the kidneys and bladder. Too much uric acid in the urine. A tendency to consumption.

Saturn, Uranus or Neptune in Libra.—Impure blood, strangury, pains in the knees and back, sometimes a touch of sciatica or gout.

Saturn, Uranus or Neptune in Scorpio.—Sometimes depression caused through liverishness or biliousness, general malaise; hemorrhoids; derangement of the nervous system; genital organ troubles. There will be heart trouble.

Saturn, Uranus or Neptune in Sagittarius.—Pains in the hips, and sciatic nerves. A touch of rheumatism in the hips. A tendency to consumption.

Saturn, Uranus or Neptune in Capricorn.—Pains in the head; stomach trouble, indigestion and ague.

Saturn, Uranus or Neptune in Aquarius.—Pains in the joints, a touch of rheumatism, sometimes a sore throat, headaches and slight deafness.

Saturn, Uranus or Neptune in Pisces.—Much liability to chills and colds on the chest which should not be neglected; colds often taken through the feet; catarrh. Liability to consumption.

☉ ☌, ⚹, □, △ or ☍ ♂ Promittor.

Mars in Aries.—Pains in the head, insomnia.
Mars in Taurus.—Throat troubles and derangement of the kidneys.
Mars in Gemini.—Skin eruptions through impurities of the blood, feverishness and strangury.
Mars in Cancer.—Indigestion, pains in the stomach, sometimes a stomach cough.
Mars in Leo.—Heart palpitations, pains in the knees caused through the spinal-nerve; gravel and kidney disorders.
Mars in Virgo.—Constipation, bowel weakness, biliousness; sometimes worms in children.
Mars in Libra.—Kidney disorders.
Mars in Scorpio.—Pains in the head, bladder trouble, venereal distempers, ulcers. Some heart trouble.
Mars in Scorpio.—Menorrhagia, profuse and irregular menstruation, trouble with the sexual organs.
Mars in Sagittarius.—Slight feverish condition: much heat in the mouth and throat, sometimes eruptions and ulcers; pains in the hips and thighs.
Mars in Capricorn.—Trouble with the knees and ham-strings or goutish humours.
Mars in Aquarius.—Feverish distempers; pains in the limbs; heart palpitation.
Mars in Pisces.—Trouble with the feet, bowels and respiratory organs.

☉ ☌, ⚹, □, △ or ☍ ♂, ♄, ♅ or ♆ Promittors.

Sun in Aries.—Sometimes bilious or nervous headaches, feverish distempers.
Sun in Aries in the 6th.—Head troubles.
Sun in Taurus.—Throat troubles, sometimes quinsy; pains in the back and loins.
Sun in Gemini.—A feverish condition of the blood, consequently skin eruptions; weakness in the limbs.
Sun in Cancer.—Disordered stomach; a poor state and impurity of the blood. Be careful as to diet.
Sun in Leo.—Pains in the head and back; kidney disorders; feverishness.
Sun in Virgo.—Bowel and stomach trouble; sometimes a sore throat.
Sun in Libra.—Venereal distempers; kidney derangement; a touch of rheumatism in the arms and shoulders; an over-heated condition of the blood.
Sun in Scorpio.—Amenorrhœa. Arrested or obstructed menstruation, trouble with the genital organs. Heart trouble.
Sun in Scorpio.—Stomach, kidney and urinal troubles; trouble with the sexual organs.

Sun in Sagittarius.—Fistula, ulcers of the leg (ulceration is nature's way of curing certain diseases), feverish distempers; a liability to swooning.

Sun in Capricorn.—Bowel and stomach troubles. Sometimes lameness in the knees.

Sun in Aquarius.—Strangury. Kidney disorders; heart palpitation, over-heated blood; pains in the back.

Sun in Pisces.—Genital organ and bowel troubles. A touch of strangury.

☽ ☌, ⚹, ◻, ⃞ OR ☍ ♂, ♄, ♆ OR ♅ PROMITTORS.

Moon in Aries.—Catarrh. Lethargy; headaches.
Moon in Taurus.—Throat troubles; pains in the limbs.
Moon in Gemini.—A touch of gout; trouble with the respiratory organs.
Moon in Cancer.—Stomach derangement; epilepsy, a poor state of the blood; flatulence; sometimes a collection of watery fluid.
Moon in Leo.—Heart palpitation. A little throat trouble; pains in the back.
Moon in Virgo.—Bowel and stomach troubles. Never neglect a cold which may fly to the bowels and produce an inflammatory distemper. Depression through biliousness, or nervous debility.
Moon in Libra.—Kidney and stomach troubles. Back weakness, liability to pleurisy.
Moon in Libra.—Leucorrhœa. Catarrh of the womb.*
Moon in Scorpio.—Urinary and genital organ trouble; kidney distempers. Heart palpitation. Swoonings after over-exertion.
Moon in Scorpio.—Amenorrhœa or dysmenorrhœa.*
Moon in Sagittarius.—Distempers in the bowels. Weakness in the limbs. Be careful as to diet.
Moon in Capricorn.—Kidney troubles; back weakness; a touch of gout.
Moon in Capricorn.—Leucorrhœa. Catarrh of the womb.*
Moon in Aquarius.—Bladder trouble and a tendency to hysteria. Nervous disorders; pains in the limbs. A little heart trouble.
Moon in Pisces.—A poor state of the blood; colds taken through the feet; an accumulation of watery fluid.

☿ IN THE 6TH HOUSE AND ☌, ⚹, ◻, ⃞, OR ☍ ♂, ♄, ♅ OR ♆.

Mercury in Aries.—Head trouble, vertigo; noises in the head may arise from indigestion and excesses of any kind.
Mercury in Taurus.—Throat trouble. Hoarseness.
Mercury in Gemini.—Varicose. Headaches.
Mercury in Cancer.—Stomach troubles; indigestion.
Mercury in Leo.—Palpitation. Pains in the back.

* Female's Horoscope.

Mercury in Virgo.—Flatulence. Colic. Pains in the head; distempers in the bowels.

Mercury in Libra.—Derangement of the kidneys. Be careful as to diet because of urinal obstructions.

Mercury in Scorpio.—Distempers in the bowels. Trouble with the sexual organs; a touch of rheumatism.

Mercury in Sagittarius.—Kidney and stomach trouble; weakness in the back; a little derangement of the nervous system.

Mercury in Capricorn.—Imperfect filtration of urine. Goutish humours. Pains in the knees and back; depression.

Mercury in Aquarius.—A touch of rheumatism. Bowel trouble.

Mercury in Pisces.—Kidney trouble; pains in the head; distempers in the genital organs, sometimes a little lung weakness.

Various Evil Aspects of Promittors.

Mercury in adverse aspect to Mars.—Slight cuts to the hands and arms.

Sun or Moon in evil aspect to Mars.—Hurts, falls, accidents, feverish distempers or inflammation; also ruptures.

Mars in evil aspect to Saturn.—Accidents, wounds and hurts.

Mars on the ascendant.—Slight hurts and cuts, especially to the head and face.

Moon in conjunction with the Pleiades on the western angle.—Infirmities of sight; or weak sight.

Jupiter afflicted. Sun in adverse aspect to Jupiter.—Liverishness; stomach troubles; an indifferent or impure state of the blood.

Venus afflicting the Moon.—Occasional indisposition.

Mars in good aspect to the Sun.—Great strength of constitution. The spark of vitality is not easily extinguished. You have a huge store of vitality to draw upon in hours of sickness.

Saturn in adverse aspect to the Sun from common signs.—Your circulation and vitality are not very good.

Horoscopes of Women marked "F." (female).

F. *Sun in Scorpio in adverse aspect to Neptune, Uranus or Saturn.*—Painful and imperfect menstruation (dysmenorrhœa) and anæmia.

F. *Sun in Taurus, Leo or Aquarius afflicted by Uranus, Neptune or Saturn.*—Tends to imperfect menstruation (amenorrhœa) or profuse menstruation (menorrhagia). When there is profuse menstruation there is much liability to leucorrhœa and anæmia.

F. *Moon in Taurus, Scorpio, Leo or Aquarius, afflicted by Saturn, Uranus or Neptune.*—Dysmenorrhœa, leucorrhœa or amenorrhœa.

F. *Sun in Scorpio or Taurus, afflicted by Mars, Uranus or Saturn.*—Immoderate menstrual discharges or dysmenorrhœa.

When Jupiter is an adverse Promittor.

Jupiter in adverse aspect to the Sun in Aries.—Causes blood impurity, consequently headaches.

Jupiter in adverse aspect to the Sun in Taurus.—Indicates goutish humours, a little throat trouble.

Jupiter in adverse aspect to the Sun in Gemini.—Causes blood impurity.

Jupiter in adverse aspect to the Sun in Cancer.—Causes indigestion, liverishness, blood impurity.

Jupiter in adverse aspect to the Sun in Leo.—Causes heart palpitation.

Jupiter in adverse aspect to the Sun in Virgo.—Causes bowel, liver and lung troubles.

Jupiter in adverse aspect to the Sun in Libra.—Causes blood impurity; tumours are to be feared.

Jupiter in adverse aspect to the Sun in Scorpio.—Causes urinal trouble.

Jupiter in adverse aspect to the Sun in Sagittarius.—Causes blood impurity, feverishness.

Jupiter in adverse aspect to the Sun in Capricorn.—Causes depression, throat trouble.

Jupiter in adverse aspect to the Sun in Aquarius.—Causes blood impurity, lumbago.

Jupiter in adverse aspect to the Sun in Pisces.—Causes dropsical humours, blood impurity.

CHAPTER XII.

MENTAL QUALITIES AND DISPOSITION.

It is a well-known fact that no two persons possessing the same characteristics are born under different signs of the Zodiac, and it is very easy to pick out the different types in one's own circle.

The Sagittary man, or the person at whose birth this sign ascends, is as far removed in character as the poles from the person at whose birth the sign Taurus, Cancer or Capricorn held the ascendant. This invariability is of itself sufficient evidence that nature does not evolve a jumble of conflicting atoms. Compare the timid, reserved, fearful, retiring, suspicious person, whose birth moment coincides with Saturn's ascension in the eastern horizon, with the native at whose birth Jupiter presides.

The latter's honest bluntness, bonhomie, generosity, free and open disposition, and sport-loving temperament, are a striking contrast to the former.

The bold, self-confident, self-assertive, quarrelsome individual at whose birth Mars was in evidence, is a sharp contrast to the person owning Venus as mistress.

The latter's love of peace, fondness of pleasure, vivacity, warmth of affection and fun-loving temperament, are a striking contrast to the Saturnine man's physical condition.

Ptolemy tells us that the mental and intellectual qualities are judged from the condition of ☿ and also from the luminaries (particularly the Moon) and their aspects.

Certain it is that the greatest of all clairvoyants, Swedenborg, was born January 29th, 1688, at 5.30 a.m., just as the benevolent Jupiter with Venus rose in the eastern horizon in trine aspect with the Moon. Saturn had culminated for the day; Mercury was also in the ascendant.

These positions, in the language of the heavens, portray a gifted man, possessing rare talents; but as Mercury was in quartile aspect with both the malefics, Mars and Saturn, he had undoubtedly that insanity which is often allied to genius and inspiration.

The place of Mercury, aspects to Mercury, the ascendant, planets therein, or in the 1st house, the 10th, the 3rd, and 9th houses are all to be observed in judging the mind; for all these places are spiritual, brain or mind swaying and controlling.

♊, ♍, ♎ and ♒ on the ascendant incline the native to intellectual work. And if ☿ be rising in these signs, the native is clever, unless ☿ be afflicted.

☿ rising in any sign, unafflicted, adds some good abilities.

☿ in good aspect to ♃ gives the native superior judgment and reasoning powers. The aspect of ♂ to ☿ sharpens the wit and adds constructive skill.

The conjunction or good aspects between ☿ and the ☽ add more than ordinary sharpness of wit and intuition.

The good aspects of ♄ and ♅ to ☿ beget imagination, subtlety, penetration of mind. The evil aspects of ♄ to ☿ beget a person of dull wit. Whilst the cross aspects of the ☽ and ♂, beget stupidity.

A conjunction of the ☉ and ☿ adds a practical judgment, sharpness of wit.

♀ or ♃ rising adds benevolence of disposition, kindliness.

But see planets rising and aspects thereto.

Those who have ☿ in good aspect to ♀ have usually artistic, or musical ability, and if ♀ is in good aspect to ♆ and ♂ the abilities are superior. These aspects are often found in the horoscopes of composers. Those who have ☿ in good aspect to ♂ have astuteness, quickness of intellect. The mind is keen, penetrating, tart, and if ☿ is in adverse aspect to Mars the wit may be intense but caustic and often violent. The good aspect of ☿ and ♃ is productive of the highest gift of reasoning—the exercise of great thoughts. The reasonable thinking leads to study and wisdom. It is the aspect of great intelligence and enlightenment. ☿ in good aspect to ♅ adds originality of ideas, inventive skill, and some degree of power of penetration.

CHAPTER XIII.

PECUNIARY PROSPECTS.

. . . "And even at this day,
'Tis Jupiter who brings whate'er is great."

GEORGE ELIOT says: "Babies can't choose their own horoscopes, and, indeed, if they could, there might be an inconvenient rush of babies at particular epochs."

As Saturn passes through the 2nd house once every twenty-four hours, and for many days each year, conjoins, squares and opposes the Sun and Moon, it will readily be seen that thousands are born every year who are destined to come to actual want. Unfortunate horoscopes are largely in excess of the good horoscopes.

Astrologers have recorded that Saturn in the 2nd house (that division of the heaven which presides over pecuniary affairs), in conjunction, square, or opposition to either or both the luminaries or planets, is a sure sign of poverty, if the Sun and Moon are found in adverse aspect to each other.*

Milton had Saturn in the 2nd house, and his perpetual struggle to live is well known.

Those who have at birth Jupiter or the Sun in the 2nd house or the mid-heaven, in good aspect to each other or the Moon, accumulate wealth. Coleridge was born 11 a.m., October 21st, 1772; at his birth the Sun was in the 10th house, in trine aspect with Jupiter in the 2nd house. M. Carnot was born 6 p.m., August 11th, 1837; Jupiter and the Sun will be found conjoined in the western angle, both in trine aspect with the Moon. George Eliot, born 5 a.m., November 22nd, 1819, had the Sun in the same position in good aspect to Mars, Saturn and the Moon.

A ✶ or △ aspect of the luminaries is a sure sign of good fortune in business, and if either are in the 10th or 2nd house, much pecuniary success.

* It will be observed that the malefic planets exceed the good planets by two to one, which means that there is and must be a large number of very unfortunate people in the world.

♀ in the 2nd, well-aspected, brings much money gain.

Of course ♃ or ♀ in the 2nd, in cross aspect to the luminaries or malefics, would keep the native poor.

♂ in the 2nd causes extravagance, rash business ventures; mutations of fortune, if Mars is well-aspected; if ill-aspected, the native will be poor. The good aspects of ♃ to ♅, ♄, or ♆ bring legacies, inheritances; an independence from these sources.

♆, ♄, ♂, or ♅ in evil aspect to one or both luminaries, and either malefics or luminaries in the 5th, presage heavy losses in speculations and bad investments.

Good aspects of ♀ and ♃ to ☿ bring gain by intellectual capacity. That is to say, the native makes money by his abilities. Teachers and schoolmasters generally have ☿ in the 10th house.

The aspects which portray success in business are ☽ ⊻ ☉, ☽ 36° ☉, ☽ ✶ ☉, ☽ Q ☉, ☽ Bq. ☉, and ☽ △ ☉. They bring money. ☽ ✶ ♃, ☽ Bq. ♃, ☽ △ ♃ are also aspects which bring extraordinary good fortune and much money. Those who have such aspects are lucky. ☉ ✶ ♃, ☉ Q ♃, ☉ Bq. ♃, and ☉ △ ♃, bring much good fortune. ☽ ✶ ♀, ☽ ☌ ♀, ☽ △ ♀, bring a modicum of success. ☽ ☌ ☿, ☽ ✶ ☿, ☽ Bq. ☿, and ☽ △ ☿, bring success as the result of ability and mental efforts. ☽ ✶ ♂, ☽ Bq. ♂, and ☽ △ ♂, bring much success as the result of energy—physical and mental activity.

Mercury sextile Jupiter, Mercury conjunction Jupiter, Mercury Bq. Jupiter, or Mercury trine Jupiter.—Brings success by talents, abilities—success in scientific work, literature—it is the aspect of the scholar, the philosopher and man of letters, the journalist.

Mercury sextile Mars, Mercury Bq. Mars, or Mercury trine Mars.—This is also the aspect of the man who succeeds by his sharpness of wit, his mental energy, ability, constructive skill, and often his journalistic ability, or as a lawyer or barrister.

Mercury conjunction Venus, Mercury sextile Venus, or Mercury semi-sextile Venus.—This is also the aspect which confers literary ability, musical talent. It is the aspect often found in the horoscope of the scholar, musician, composer, journalist. Those who are fortunate enough to be born at a moment when Mercury receives the good aspects of Jupiter, Mars, Venus, and the Moon are indeed highly gifted. Such horoscopes are rare, for such a person would be a genius if Mercury was found in the ascendant and the hereditary abilities were also good. But of course uncommon powers of intellect may come from parents and the superior combination of hereditary and planetary intelligence completes the faculty, even though but one or two aspects are formed to Mercury.

Of course aspects of Uranus, Saturn and Neptune to Mercury when they are the sextile, Bq. or trine, add abilities which enable a man to accomplish much. Such men have ability for the study of science, mathematics, and if the inherited endowment is superior, then inventive and constructive skill of a very high order would result from the union.

When Mercury is afflicted by the malefics, such as Mars, the wit is sharpened; but when Saturn is the afflicting planet then the wit is clouded. Of course, if there is superior inherited ability then the fusion with poor horoscopical faculty through a badly afflicted Mercury, may mean that the man will display a good deal of mental power and may achieve much, since it is admitted that what is transmitted by descent from parents or grandparents is more potent than what is conferred by the aspects to Mercury in the horoscope.

When the Moon is found in adverse aspect to the Sun the person should never embark in risky business ventures, and if the Moon is afflicted by Saturn and receives no support from Jupiter, then much ill-luck and heavy losses are to be expected. Unfortunate people who lose money in business have invariably the luminaries in cross aspect to each other, or the Moon afflicted by Saturn. The most unlucky horoscopes, therefore, financially are those which have the Sun and Moon in cross aspect and the Moon afflicted by Saturn. Those who have the Moon afflicted by Saturn but supported by a good aspect from Jupiter will meet with much good fortune, because the good aspect of Jupiter modifies the evil influence of Saturn.

We have found men with the Moon afflicted by Saturn but in good aspect to Jupiter, and they have met with much success. Those with good and bad aspects meet with mutations of fortune, that is to say, they make money and lose money. When the bad aspects outnumber the good aspects, then the person meets with some ugly twists of Fortune's wheel; when he gets hold of the money he has difficulty in retaining it. When the good and bad aspects are equal it is also difficult to accumulate money, and yet a person with such aspects will get an independence.

Those who have Mercury in good aspect to Jupiter will make money by their abilities, and the same remark applies to a good aspect of Venus to Mercury. Ability therefore. is a valuable asset, and the more numerous the good aspects formed to Mercury the greater is the intellectual asset. The good aspect of the Sun to Mercury indicates much capacity for business, much executive power and consequent success. The good aspect of Mars to Mercury enables people to make money in journalism, politics, chemistry and legal work. Such people do well in avocations requiring sharpness of wit, they have great mental energy, and if there is no physical impediment they will accomplish much in some department of human knowledge. We have observed men with indifferent abilities, illiterate in many cases, but they have made much money, they have been very lucky; but the luminaries have been in good aspect to each other and the Moon in good aspect to Jupiter. Therefore, some men succeed by their abilities, which may be horoscopical or from hereditary sources, others by their luck. Whilst the latter is always known by reference to the horoscope, the former is not unless one can inspect the horoscopes of parents and grandparents. It must not be forgotten that those who have undesirable horoscopical qualities injure their fortune by bad personal conduct, by bad habits, dishonesty and untrustworthiness. When a person whose fortunes depend upon his abilities is guilty of misconduct, his position is indeed an unenviable one.

When Mars is in the ascendant and in adverse aspect to Saturn, that person may, in a moment of misfortune, take his own life. We know of one case where heavy money loss caused a man to commit suicide, and in another case an accusation of cruelty caused the person to kill himself.

A person with Saturn rising in adverse aspect to Venus may bring himself into social disrepute by unlawful acts and vicious conduct.

The interpretation of the fortunes is one of the most difficult subjects of Astrology; but it may be safely said that in difficult cases where the luminaries are in cross aspect and afflicted by the malefics, and if Mercury is receiving good aspects, the intellectual road is the only road which will lead to success. Happy and successful indeed is he who has Mercury well-aspected, whilst the luminaries are found in good aspect to each other, and in good aspect to Jupiter, with no hostile aspects from Saturn, Uranus or Neptune. The good aspects of the malefics to Mercury certainly enable the person to go far in the study of science and literature, and they are a great aid to success.

CHAPTER XIV.

THE EMPLOYMENT.

If the Moon is in good aspect to the Sun, such an aspect is sure to bring a good deal of business success. A good aspect of the Moon to Jupiter also brings much good-luck; it is essentially the aspect of much good fortune.

The good aspects of the Sun to Venus and Mercury also indicate much business success.

Of course, if the Moon is free from the adverse aspect of Saturn and is in good aspect to the Sun, a business career should be chosen. If the Moon is not in good aspect to the Sun and Jupiter, and Mercury is in good aspect to Jupiter or Venus, then the intellectual road should be taken, it will lead to success.

If Jupiter is in the 9th house the Church or Ministry for a profession is an eminently desirable one.

Good aspects of Mars to the Sun beget good soldiers, surgeons, or engineers.

Of course the more good aspects Mercury receives the greater the success in literature, art, science, chemistry, or as a lawyer or barrister. It is essential that Mercury should be free from the cross aspects of Saturn, Neptune and Uranus for great success to attend mental efforts, for cross aspects of these planets not only dull the intellect, but they cause eccentricity, sometimes ill-directed efforts—yet cross aspects from the malefics will not spoil the intellect if Mercury has good aspects of Venus, Jupiter and the Moon. A lawyer should certainly have a good aspect of Mercury to Jupiter, just as an artist or musician should have good aspects of Venus, Mercury, Mars and Neptune. Accountants and engineers should have Mercury in good aspect to Mars.

Gemini, Virgo or Libra on the ascendant are intellectual signs, that is to say they impart a certain amount of intellectual ability, just as Venus rising adds a certain amount of artistic ability.

Barristers, or those who require extreme sharpness of wit, should have one of the intellectual signs on the ascendant and Mercury in good aspect to Mars and Venus, the Moon should also be in good aspect to Mercury.

Those who seek office under Municipal Authorities or under Government should if possible have Jupiter or the Sun on the Meridian receiving favourable aspects. Venus there is also of happy augury.

Good aspects of Jupiter and the Moon to the Sun are favourable for success as Bankers and if the Moon is in good aspect to the Sun they may become merchant princes should the Moon be free from the affliction of Saturn. The horoscope of Mr. C. Arthur Pearson is a very good example of a successful financial magnate, but there are very few horoscopes so entirely propitious as his.

It will be observed that Mercury, the Sun and Venus are angular, that is to say they are on the Meridian, and they are all in trine to the Moon. Mr. Pearson has not only good-luck dogging his footsteps but he has ability, and when the horoscope bestows superior abilities and great prosperity then such a man is sure to achieve great things and become very powerful. As the toll which industry exacts during a single year is heavy (it is over one hundred and twenty thousand a year; that is to say that number of persons meet with injuries in their various avocations and over a thousand are killed), it is of the utmost importance that those who have the Sun or Moon in adverse aspect to Mars, or that planet on the ascendant (which is the cause of death by accident and injuries), should select that employment which is the least dangerous.

♄ inclines to building, farming.

♃ represents priests, clergymen, bankers, lawyers, merchants, persons in powerful positions.

♂ indicates soldiers, surgeons, engineers, butchers, mechanics.

♀ indicates musicians, artists, jewellers, actors, drapers.

The ☉ indicates officials; that is municipal or government officers, and those in powerful positions.

☿ represents mathematicians, secretaries, literary and scientific men, schoolmasters.

☽ indicates the people, the multitude, travellers, sailors.

For instance, ♄ in either the upper or lower meridian, well-aspected, would bring success in farming, building.

♃ there and well-aspected, the native would do well as a banker, lawyer, merchant.

♂ in either position would indicate success in chemistry, engineering and the employments over which he presides.

But all these planets should be well aspected by the Sun.

The planet nearest the Sun, or in aspect to the mid-heaven, has some power in directing the native's employment.

If ♂ is near the ☉, some of the martial employments will probably be taken up. But the dominant planets in the horoscope have considerable influence in this matter.

For instance, ☉ ☌ ♀ would incline to a drapery or jewellery business. And if this conjunction occurred in the 3rd or 9th, the native would do well as a commercial traveller or importer.

Generally speaking, editors should have good aspects between the ☽, ☿, ♀ and ♃.

Artists should have good aspects between ♀ and ☿, ♀ and ♂; musicians also should have these aspects and ♀ in the 10th or ascendant.

A successful soldier should have ☉ in good aspect to ♂ and one or both angular.

The lawyer should have a good aspect between ♃ and ☿.

Clergymen should have ♃ or ♀ in the 9th, or the ☉ there well aspected by ♃.

People in public offices should have ♃ on the M.C.

Surgeons should have good aspects between the ☉, ☿ and ♂.

CHAPTER XV.

MARRIAGE.

The planet or planets to which the ☽ applies in the horoscope of a male, represents the wife.

For instance: if the ☽ applies to ♂, the wife is self-assertive, confident, wilful.

If to ♀, she is kindly, affectionate, lovable.

If to ♄, cold, reserved, reticent.

If to ♃, attractive, faithful; a good woman.

The ☉ in the horoscope of a female is a significator. Observe the planet to which the Sun applies and with which it is about to form an aspect, for that is the planet which will be found prominent if not the actual ruler of the husband. The same remarks apply to the ☽ in the horoscope of a man.

If applying to a good aspect of ♃, the husband is good-natured, affectionate, and a good man.

If to ♄, he is reserved. If the good aspect is to ♂, the man is self-assertive, confident, bold, generous.

Evil aspects to the luminaries cause unhappy marriages, conflicts, widowhood.

A planet on the western angle must be taken as an indicator of the marriage partner; it has precedence to the planet or planets to which the luminaries apply.

♀ afflicted by ♄, the woman rarely marries, unless the ☉ is supported by ♃; disappointment in love is certain if the ☉ and ♀ be afflicted by ♄, ♅ or ♆.

♄, ♅ or ♆ on the western angle will keep a woman single, unless ♃ is in good aspect to the ☉. Then she may marry, but any of these planets on the western angle always cause domestic infelicity. The trouble in the married life is greater if one of these planets be on the western angle and in cross aspects to other planets. Even ♃ or ♀ on the western angle can only bring domestic felicity when they are unaspected, or well-aspected.

For if they are afflicted the man or woman is unhappily married.

As to the period of marriage: in the case of a male, any aspect of the promittor, the ☽ to the planet to which it applied at birth, or to any planet on the western angle, will bring about marriage, if the native has reached a marriageable age.

In the horoscope of a female, the ☉ as the promittor must be taken in the same way.

In a woman's horoscope if the Sun is afflicted by Neptune or applying to an adverse aspect of Neptune the husband will be captious, uncertain, peculiar, singular and resentful in temper.

If the Sun is applying to an adverse aspect of Saturn the husband will be selfish, exacting, reticent, taciturn; he may drink and neglect his wife.

The Sun afflicted by Mars, the husband will be severe, cruel, bold, rash, aggressive, often unreasonable, masterful. He may be fond of drink and follow dissolute ways.

When the Sun is afflicted by Uranus the husband is rather queer, capricious, most irregular, critical in temper.

When Venus and the Sun are afflicted by the malefics in the horoscope of a woman she very rarely marries if one of the malefics occupies the Western Angle, for there is much difficulty in finding a suitable mate; similarly, when the Moon and Venus in the horoscope of a man are afflicted by Saturn and Saturn is on the Western Angle the man will have a disinclination to marry.

The Sun in good aspect to Uranus the husband will be independent in character, studious, rather eccentric.

The Sun in good aspect to Jupiter or Venus the husband will be kind, affectionate, generous, just, possessing a good disposition.

The Sun in good aspect to Mars makes the husband generous, self-assertive, rather wilful but bold, energetic.

The Sun in good aspect to Saturn makes the husband grave, careful, sometimes rather shy, industrious, acquisitive, constant in attachment, fond of his home.

The Sun in good aspect to Mercury makes the husband clever, fond of science or literature, or an active man of business.

The Moon in good aspect to Mercury will make the wife clever, sharp, active, sensible, intellectual, intuitive but probably talkative.

The Moon in good aspect to Venus the wife will be fond of music, art; she will probably be clever, refined, amiable, pleasure-loving, kind-hearted, vivacious and affectionate.

The Moon in good aspect to Mars the wife will be daring, active, bold, disliking control, self-assertive, confident, optimistic.

The Moon in good aspect to Saturn the wife will be rather reserved she will take life seriously and will be retiring, constant in attachment. If the Moon is in evil aspect to Saturn she will be at times morose, peevish, selfish, malicious, often suffering in health if Saturn is on the Western Angle.

The Moon in adverse aspect to Mars the wife will be masterful, wilful, rash, excitable, quarrelsome, unreasonable.

The Moon in good aspect to Jupiter portrays the best of wives; she will be generous, cheerful, affectionate, kind-hearted, sympathetic. She will be indulgent to her offspring and her husband.

The Moon in good aspect to Uranus will make the wife independent in character.

The Moon in good aspect to the Sun will make the wife proud, firm, high-minded, self-confident, with a commanding presence and much force of character.

In the horoscope of a woman the good aspect between the luminaries would make the husband gentle, quiet, fond of travelling, and a good man. When the Sun is afflicted by the malefics in the horoscope of a woman and a malefic is on the Western Angle sickness or death of the husband is to be feared.

Of course the ☉'s aspect to other than the planets it aspects at birth often brings about marriage.

♀ afflicted by ♄, ♅ or ♆, indicates trouble in love affairs.

Aspects between ♂ and ♀ beget love affairs.

Evil aspects of ♂, ♆ and ♅ to the ☽ often cause much disquietude in the married life, and sometimes divorce or separation results.

When the ☽ applies to ♂ in the horoscope of a male, it does not necessarily mean that ♂ must be in the ascendant. It merely means that ♂ will be dominant in the wife's horoscope, and that the martial nature will be strong within her.

A good aspect between the husband's ☽ and the wife's ☉ is a sign of concord.

Aspects between ♀ and ♂ in the respective horoscopes cause love; the one fascinates the other.

The Offspring.

The 5th and 11th houses indicate the offspring. ♅, ♂, ♄ in these houses and in cross aspects often deny offspring.

♄ in the 5th afflicting the ☉ is a sure indication of the death of some of the offspring. ♂ in the 5th afflicting either of the luminaries often kills the native's children; ♂ there is sure to cause trouble from offspring—they are difficult to control; ♃ or ♀ there, good, happy and obedient offspring.

Twins.

We have found that twins born within a few minutes and having almost the same ascending degree have differed very much in character and temperament. They have been found to be very dissimilar in strength of constitution.

One has inherited the father's character and physical strength, whilst the other has inherited the mother's traits of character and delicacy of constitution. These twins were swayed by inherited faculties which impelled them to follow different walks of life. They inherited inclinations which were entirely diverse and which caused their lives to be entirely different.

CHAPTER XVI.

TRAVELLING.

The Moon in the 1st, 12th, 3rd or 9th houses is a sure sign of long journeys and voyages. If the ☽ is well aspected, and there are no evil planets in the 3rd or 9th, good fortune would come from journeys; but especially if the 3rd or 9th are occupied by ♀ or ♃, and they are in good aspect to the luminaries.

Evil planets in the 9th, and afflicting the ☉ or ☽, the malice of fortune will result from journeys, which should be avoided. Generally the native will do best by going in the direction in which he finds the benefics in the horoscope. For instance: if ♃ is in the 9th, he should go a little south-west from birth-place; if the luminaries on the western angle are well aspected, he could go west; ♀ ☌ ☉ in the 3rd, he would do well in a north-easterly direction.

But we have always found it unfortunate for a person to go to a place ruled by a sign which is occupied in his horoscope by an afflicted planet, even though it be a benefic; and that the evil would be increased if, at the time of moving, a malefic was found transiting that planet's place. ♃, ♀ or the Sun or ☽ in the 9th house and receiving good aspects or in good aspect to each other indicate much success in other lands, and the further the person goes the better he will fare. ♃ in the 9th and in good aspect to the ☽ and if the ☽ is in good aspect to the Sun will bring immense prosperity abroad.

The ☽ in the 9th and well aspected, but especially if in good aspect to the Sun, brings good fortune in other lands.

We believe the following list of places ruled by the twelve signs to be not entirely unreliable.

♈. Germany, England and Wales, Denmark, Lesser Poland, Burgundy, Palestine, Syria, Judæa, Naples, Capua, Florence, Verona, Padua, Brunswick, Marseilles, Cracow, Saragossa, Utrecht.

♉. Persia, Ireland, Cyprus, Poland, Dublin, Mantua, Leipsic.

♊. Lombardy, Belgium, North America, London, Versailles, Bruges, Nuremberg, and Melbourne.

♋. Western Africa, Scotland, Holland, Amsterdam, Constantinople, Cadiz, Genoa, Venice, Algiers, Tunis, York, New York, Milan, Lubeck, and Manchester; perhaps Vincenza, Magdeburg, and Rochdale.

♌. France, Italy, Sicily, the Alps, Bohemia, Chaldea, North of Roumania, Rome, Bath, Bristol, Taunton, Damascus, Prague, Philadelphia.

♍. Turkey, Asia, Babylonia, Assyria, Euphrates, Greece, Thessaly, Corinth, Candia, Croatia, Switzerland, Heidelburg, Jerusalem, Paris, Reading, Lyons, Toulouse, Cheltenham.

♎. Thibet, China, Japan, Austria, Savoy, Upper Egypt, Libya, Antwerp, Frankfort, Lisbon, Spires, Fribourg, Vienna, Gaëta, Charlestown, Placenza.

♏. Morocco, Algiers, Barbary, Norway, Bavaria, Valentia, Frankfort-on-the-Oder, Halifax, Liverpool.

♐. Spain, Tuscany, Arabia, Felix, Dalmatia, Hungary, Moravia, Cologne, Avignon, Buda, Narbonne, Toledo, Rotenburg, Stuttgart.

♑. India, Afghanistan, Punjaub, Thrace, Macedonia, The Morea, Bosnia, Bulgaria, Albania, West Saxony, Hesse, Mexico, Mecklenburg, Prato in Tuscany, Brandenburg, Tortona, Brussels.

♒. Arabia, Russia, Prussia, Tartary, Muscovy, Circassia, Wallachia, Sweden, Westphalia, Abyssinia, Hamburg, Bremen, Salzburg.

♓. Portugal, Calabria, Normandy, Egypt, Nubia, Alexandria, Ratisbon.

We confess that our experience has failed to verify that all the towns and countries mentioned are ruled by the twelve signs. The student, therefore, is warned that much may be disproved by demonstrational evidence of research. Great caution, therefore, is necessary in so difficult a subject, as "where to go to find good fortune."

CHAPTER XVII.

FRIENDS AND ENEMIES.

The 11th house is indicative of friends; the Sun, Moon, Jupiter, and Venus therein, unafflicted, prefigure many good and powerful friends, who will contribute to the native's happiness and good fortune. The writer has known of cases where friends have assisted the native to lucrative positions and favours. Jupiter, Venus, the Sun, and Moon, afflicted by cross or opposition aspects, however, in the 11th house, would bring trouble rather than help from friends. Mars, Saturn, or Uranus, or even Neptune, in this house, would bring loss from false and aggressive friends, who turn enemies.

The 7th house indicates open or public enemies, and the 12th house alludes to the secret or private scheming foes. Saturn, Uranus, Mars, or Neptune, in these houses, instigate enemies, and stir up strife, if they are in cross or opposition aspect to each other or either of the luminaries. Planets opposing each other from the east and western angles cause powerful opposition (often litigation) from ever-contending foes. Jupiter, or Venus, or the Sun, in the 7th house, opposed or squared, are also productive of litigation, disputes, a thwarting influence from people in strong positions. The more numerous the aspects from the east and western angles, the greater the conflicts; for the native, under these circumstances, finds large sections of the public opposed to him.

The malefics, Saturn, Uranus, and Mars, in the 12th house, squared or opposed, are positive tokens of false charges, accusations difficult to trace; they portend plots of backbiters, assaults in the dark, assassinations. Find Mars in the 12th house in conjunction, square or opposition, and the neighbours will speak ill of the native. Good aspects to the Sun, Jupiter, and Venus, in the 7th, make the native popular; he has many followers and admirers. A certain attractive influence is attributed to the 12th house when Venus and Jupiter are so posited. An Arabian astrologer says that ♀ in the 12th makes a man wise and good; but this could only be the case if Venus was found near the ascendant, or actually in the ascendant. However, he may be right in assuming that since a malefic causes antipathy, a benefic will cause sympathy.

The Sun, Venus, Jupiter, or ☿ in the 11th house, and in good aspect with each other, indicate much gain by friends—often advancement and help from influential friends if ♃ or the Sun are in the 11th house and in good aspect to each other or to the ☽, ♀ or ☿.

CHAPTER XVIII.

STAR COURSES.

SOLAR AND LUNAR ASPECTS TO PROMITTORS AND NON-PROMITTORS.

WE have found after twenty years' research (and the work has entailed the casting of thousands of horoscopes and the calculations of Star Courses) that the aspects formed by the Sun to the planets (in cases where no aspect was found in the horoscope) have often proved inoperative because they are Non-Promittors, that is to say the planets promised nothing (*i.e.*, neither good nor bad fortune in the horoscope) hence they brought next to nothing when they formed subsequent aspects to the Sun or Moon. The Star Courses, however, of Non-Promittors are not entirely devoid of influence when they form aspects to the Sun. We have found that the good aspect of the Sun to Jupiter has brought slight benefits when Jupiter formed no good aspect to the Sun in the horoscope; but when Jupiter has been found in bad aspect to the Sun his subsequent good aspect in the Star Courses has always failed to bring even slight benefits. On the other hand we have found that an adverse aspect formed by the Sun to Mars, Saturn, Uranus or Neptune, when they have formed no aspect with the Sun at birth, has caused slight losses or slight indisposition and sometimes disappointment or family trouble, and in the case of frail constitutions or aged persons a breakdown in health and death has sometimes resulted when the person has been very old and feeble.

The Moon's aspects to Non-Promittors in the Star Courses, however, have so little power that they are hardly ever productive unless Mars, Saturn, Uranus, Neptune or Jupiter are in the ascendant or angular and even in such cases they mostly fail to be influential unless two or more aspects coincide; but if a good aspect of the Moon and Jupiter coincides with a bad aspect of the Moon and Saturn then Jupiter will modify or counteract the bad influence of Saturn, whilst Jupiter is himself rendered impotent by the Saturnian ray. Of course this remark is applicable in cases of subsequent aspects of Promittors, for when the Moon simultaneously forms a good aspect with Jupiter and a bad aspect with Saturn the one planet thwarts the other—*i.e.*, both planets are rendered impotent or there may be a modicum of good and a modicum of bad fortune.

Mars, however, does not appear to possess this power to such a degree, for when Mars interposes a bad aspect to the Moon coinciding with Jupiter's good aspect Jupiter's power does not appear to be diminished to any serious extent.

We do not affirm that the aspects of Non-Promittors are entirely or altogether inoperative and that they are to be discarded, though their effects at times can scarcely be felt. We have known an attack of sickness, influenza, or money loss to coincide with cross aspects to the Sun of Non-Promittors when the horoscope has been found to be an unlucky one; whereas the Promittors never fail, whether it is the aggressive fortune of Mars, the malice of fortune of Saturn, Uranus or Neptune, or the happy fortunes of a kindly Jupiter or propitious Venus as regards their aspects to the Sun; but we confess we cannot say as much for Promittors in aspect to the Moon. Sometimes the Promittor's aspects to the Moon have proved powerfully influential and at others quite barren of results. This will be found to be the case when Jupiter is found in good aspect to the Moon at the same time that there is an adverse aspect from the malefics Saturn, Neptune, Uranus or Mars. In such cases Jupiter exerts a modifying influence.

When the Sun is assailed by more than one Malefic Promittor then the power for evil is doubled, trebled or quadrupled and life in such cases is seriously menaced; indeed, a train of evil aspects from Promittors may blast the career, cause bankruptcy or an entire breakdown in health, or death.

We have found that Solar aspects to Promittors begin to be operative two years before the completion of the aspect, sometimes two and a half and three years before completion of the aspect. Even so, the aspect is operative often for two years after the completion of the aspect. It will be seen, therefore, that Solar aspects of Promittors bring three or four years of good or bad fortune; that is to say, if it is a good aspect of the Promittor Jupiter or Venus the good influence will last for about four years, if the influence is malefic from evil Promittors it will last for four years. We may say that good and bad influences are accentuated by transits. Bad Lunar aspects coinciding with bad Solar aspects will accentuate the influence, especially if the adverse influence comes from Promittors' aspects to the Moon.

If several aspects of Non-Promittor Malefics are simultaneously formed to the Sun then a good deal of ill-fortune or ill-health may be expected. We have found that aspects from three Malefic Non-Promittors are almost as powerful for evil as one aspect of evil mien of a Promittor to the Sun, whilst a single adverse aspect of a Non-Promittor to the Sun may cause no more than a slight loss, some disappointment or a little physical debility to that part of the body which the horoscope indicates to be weak or susceptible to derangement. Though it is impossible to weigh or exactly estimate the amount of malefic influence, the more numerous the adverse aspects of Promittors or Non-Promittors, the greater will be the malice of fortune.

With regard to the power of Promittors or Non-Promittors, a Promittor has certainly 75 per cent. of adverse power whilst the adverse aspect of a Non-Promittor will bring 25 per cent. of adversity, consequently four adverse aspects of Non-Promittors would probably wreck one's fortunes.

The adverse aspects of Mars are potent and cause broils: they impel the person to undertake perilous adventures. Good aspects of Mars to the Sun often exalt the person's honour in military operations and bring authority and titular honours. But to attain these things the heroic, daring child of Mars goes through many perils, momentous incidents attended with violence and many dangers ere he wins fame. The Saturnine influence impels the person to engage in intrigues and deception: this planet will often entirely blast the person's career if Saturn is found in the Mid-heaven and in adverse aspect to the luminaries.

"STARS IN THEIR COURSES."

THE TIME MEASURE.

Solar Aspects to Promittors or Promissors.

The Chaldeans measured the span of life at the rate of a day for a year. Every degree moved by the earth in its periodical revolution in its orbit round the Sun, was reckoned one year of life.

Thus it is found that we have climacterical years; that is, years which have been found to be critical in people's lives for health and fortune. This is arrived at by multiplying seven by the odd numbers, such as three, five, seven and nine. But those who have attempted to explain these climacterical periods have failed, because they attributed some mysterious fatality to numbers. They were ignorant of arcs and angles in the celestial sphere, which are measured by degrees of longitude. We have the conjunction when two planets are conjoined; the semi-sextile of $30°$; the semi-square of $45°$; the sextile of $60°$; the quintile of $72°$; the trine of $120°$; the sesqui-quadrate of $135°$; the biquintile of $144°$; the square of $90°$; and the opposition of $180°$.

As the planets are found to exert an influence at these distances from each other, it is easy to see we have a semi-demi-arc of $90°$, equalling $22\frac{1}{2}°$; a semi-arc of the semi-sextile, equalling $15°$; and a semi-demi-arc of $7\frac{1}{2}°$.

Those who have the Sun opposed to Saturn at birth would live with difficulty through infancy, and would at age twenty-two and half suffer slightly in health; but they would be seriously ill at about age forty-five, when the Sun would have reached 135° of Saturn's radical position. Of course the arc is greater or shorter, according to the motion of Saturn.

For if Saturn turned Retrograde, he would really meet the aspect of the Sun much earlier, and possibly at age forty-two or forty-three.

We are treating of exact aspects; but should the planet Saturn be 3° past the opposition, the Sun would reach the 135° of Saturn three years earlier; the Sun's motion is sometimes over or under a degree per day.

The period of Saturn, too, must be observed. For at age seven Saturn would be in square (90°) to the Sun's place and his own place in the horoscope; and at age fifteen in conjunction with the Sun in the Radix. At age twenty-one, square Sun. At age thirty, opposition Sun. At age thirty-seven, square Sun again. At age forty-five, conjunction Sun. Therefore each of these years would be of evil mien for health and fortune.

But the degree of adversity can only be deduced from the relative positions of the Sun and Saturn in the horoscope at birth.

Of course the periodical revolution of each planet differs; and each has to be tabulated in the horoscope. For instance, the transits of Jupiter and Venus bring benefits.

For instance: Mars is sometimes Retrograde for many days, meaning many years in a person's life; because a day's progress of the planets, whether backwards or forwards, is called a year of life.

Mars is sometimes found five and six degrees beyond the 90° to the Moon, which makes a square; a most dangerous aspect, signifying aggressive fortune. The Moon at five or six months after birth completes the square; and the child meets with an accident, or is seized with convulsions, which almost wrench its life from its little body.

The transits of the afflicting planets (*i.e.*, when ♂, ♄, ♅ or ♆ are ☌, ∠, □, ⚼ or ☍ ☉) must be observed.

These aspects by transit will cause trouble or indisposition, according to the houses in which the aspects fall.

The Sun's aspects, *viz.*, ☌, ∠, □, ⚼ and ☍ to the afflicting plants, will be found to be of evil mien.

Example: We have a horoscope with the Sun in the first degree of Taurus, in opposition to Mars in the first degree of Scorpio. The Sun on January 21st, April 21st, July 24th, October 24th, would be □, ☌ or ☍ the place of Mars. In the same way the Moon's transits should be observed.

Directions tabulated in books are often misleading; for instance, it is incorrect to say that ☉ △ ♃ brings wealth and prosperity; for it will do neither unless ♃ is a promittor.

Now a promittor is a planet which promises an event.

♄, ♂, ♃, ♅, ♆, ♀ and ☿ are promittors when they aspect the luminaries.

Suppose ♃ is on the M.C. and has no aspect of the ☉, he still promises to lift the native into some position of honour. If he is ✶ ☉, then all subsequent good aspects between the ☉ and ♃ will bring good fortune.

When the ☉ reaches the Q, or a parallel, the native will benefit. Even transits of ♃ over the ☉'s place will bring benefits.

Suppose ♄ is □ ☉, closely, ♄ promises ill-health or misfortune. He fulfils his promise forty-five years later, when the ☉ comes to a ⚼ of ♄. Of course, if the ☉ is 5° beyond the exact square, then the ill-fortune would come at age forty.

Suppose the ☉ in the horoscope of a female is applying to a △ of ♃, closely, then marriage would be predicted when the ☉ comes to Bq. ♃, twenty-five years later.

Briefly, all subsequent aspects of promittors are always operative for good or evil.

The ⊻, ✶, ∠ Q or Bq. operate with great power, as powerfully as the △ or ☍.

Sometimes the luminaries are both promittors; when they are in trine or sextile aspect at birth, then prosperity in business coincides with every subsequent good aspect.

When they are in cross aspect at birth, subsequent evil aspects will continually drain a man's pecuniary resources, if he is in business.

♂ in evil aspect to the ☉ is the promittor of a particularly aggressive nature. In a woman's horoscope he sometimes kills the husband in subsequent evil aspects, such as the ∠, ⚼, □, ☍.

If it is a □ aspect at birth (close), the ⚼ obtains at age forty-five, when the event may be expected. But in the meantime ♂ is progressing often to a parallel or a ∠ of the ☉ in the radix. The student should take into consideration the houses in which the aspect falls, for these will indicate the nature of the trouble.

First ascertain what is promised in the horoscope, then follow up the subsequent aspects of promittors, and the future is revealed.

When Neptune is in evil aspect to the ☉ at birth we find that he is a particularly evil promittor. His subsequent evil aspects to the Sun bring losses and bereavement.

A married lady who had ☉ □ ♆, lost her husband forty-five years later, when the ☉ came to ⚼ ♆.

A gentleman who had the ☉ 5° past the □ of ♆, met with heavy reverses at age forty, when the ☉ came to the ⚼ of this promittor.

The system here set forth is what is usually called that of secondary or progressive directions, in which a day's movements are taken to represent a year of life, two hours for a month, thirty minutes for a week, and four minutes for a day, hence the aspects and positions formed in the first twenty-four hours after birth portray the nature of the first year of life. The ☉ by this system moves at the rate of about 1° a year.

The ☽ varies in her motion from 12° to 15° per year, hence to ascertain her motion per month we divide by twelve, and by four to show her motion per week. The ☉'s aspects to the planets are the most powerful, always producing momentous results, and never failing to bring a crisis in health or fortune. The letters R. or Rad. placed after a planet (except in the horoscope) signify the place of that planet at the time of birth, *i.e.*, in the Radix or Radical figure, which are other terms for the nativity. As before stated, this letter is also placed after the symbol of a planet in the horoscope, when it signifies that the planet is retrograde. The letter P when placed after the second of two planets in aspect refers to the second planet's progressive place, or place by secondary direction. The houses in which the direction falls must be observed, together with their lords. For instance, the ☉ or ☽□ ♄, the latter posited in the second house, would portray heavy pecuniary loss or bankruptcy. Directions from angles are very powerful, especially near the cusp of the 1st house or in the M.C. Those formed in cardinal signs are more powerful than those in fixed or common signs, and operate more suddenly. When a planet has progressed to the degree ascending at birth, or that on the mid-heaven, and at the same time forms a direction, the effects are very powerful.

The luminaries (more particularly the ☉) afflicted by ♄ in any part of the figure, bring not only ill-fortune but ill-health. We may instance the case of a male, whose ☉ in the 10th house arrived at P ♄ in the 4th; although neither the ☉ nor ♄ were lords of the 6th, 7th or 8th houses and the native had a serious illness, but did not appear to suffer in any other way.

In another case of a male, ☽ ☍ ♂ from the 3rd and 9th houses (neither of them being lord of the 6th or 8th house) brought a serious illness. Another person, whilst under ☉ ☍ ♄ and ☽ □ ♄ was seriously indisposed, and depressed by peculiar presentiments. The native broods a great deal under these last-named directions. They lead many to embrace some religious creed, more through fear of the unknown than absolute faith.

Solar Aspects to Promittors.

☉, ☌, ∠, □, ⚼, P or ☍ ♅. Changes, unsettledness, anxiety, sudden calamities, an unfortunate time for all new undertakings. The native is liable to accidents and sudden losses. In a female's natus it often causes a liaison or temptations thereto. Many leave their husbands under these directions. It sometimes causes a hasty marriage often regretted, or followed by a separation. The student must observe the houses in which the direction falls, and look for evil from things appertaining to those houses.

☉, ⊻, Sq., ⚹, Q, Bq. or △ ♅. If ♅ be prominent in a nativity this aspect brings one much into prominence. It is a good direction for municipal or parliamentary honours. It often brings beneficial changes and journeys and local distinction. Civil servants under this direction obtain rapid preferment. With females it often causes attachments or liaisons and sometimes a hasty marriage, especially if ♅ occupies the 5th or 7th house.

☉, ☌, ∠, □, ⚼, ☍ or P. ♄. This is, perhaps, the most unfortunate direction one can come under, especially for health. The □ and ☍ exert most power; the ☌, ∠ and ⚼ are not quite so strong. Death often results from this direction. When in the second house bankruptcy is almost certain to ensue. Mental anxiety, bereavement, indignities, loss of parents, grief and sorrow are generally caused by these aspects. The P. and ☌ of ☉ and ♄ in ♋, ♑ or ♒, cause rheumatism. Females often lose their husbands through these directions. A gentleman who had ♄ in the 11th house, □ ☉ and ☽, was nearly ruined by friends. When these aspects are in fixed or cardinal signs, accidents are to be feared; in watery signs, death by water or liquids.

☉, ⚺, Sq., ✶, Q, Bq. or △ ♄. Very fortunate for building or dealing in property or lands. Help from the people in whom Saturn's nature dominates, success, prosperity. These aspects incline one to be careful and accumulate property. They impart steadiness of character. With females one or other sometimes brings offers of marriage as well as good fortune.

☉, ∠, □, ⚼, or ☍ ♃. Unfortunate for finance, law, business, and speculation, especially if the aspect be from 7th, 10th, 1st, or 2nd house. It debilitates the system and liver; causing pleurisy, stomach troubles, and poor blood. The native is sure to be much abused, and to meet with injury and contumely.

☉, ☌, ⚺, Sq., ✶, Q, Bq., △ or. P. ♃. The most fortunate directions one can have. Health, honour, wealth, and prosperity; help from powerful friends. When ♃ occupies the 2nd or 10th house, during a P., ✶, or △, the native is remarkably successful in his pecuniary affairs. In a female's natus it is a sure sign of marriage or offers of marriage, if she is single and at a marriageable age.

Sun in adverse aspect to Neptune.—Presages indisposition, debility, money loss; loss in connection with changes, speculations and other money ventures. It often causes anxiety, unsettledness and unrest. Changes are generally followed by heavy reverses and sometimes bankruptcy. You will experience debility in those parts of the body in which the horoscope indicates weakness.

Sun in adverse aspect to Uranus.—Causes changes, unsettledness, loss, disappointment, indisposition and domestic infelicity. Avoid speculations and all money commitments. Look for snares and pitfalls in all business dealings. Put your savings into the safest securities, such as Consols. Take no steps on an unknown road. Entertain no overtures from others, no matter how promising they may seem.

Sun in adverse aspect to Neptune or Uranus.*—You will experience domestic

---

* In all cases where the husband is referred to or offers of marriage, the remarks are applicable to the horoscope of a female.

infelicity. These aspects often coincide with conflicts with the husband, sometimes separation. Much mental worry. Your husband's health may suffer.

Sun in adverse aspect to Saturn.—This is perhaps the most unfortunate, the most evil aspect one can come under. It has been known to assail the health, cause heavy loss, sometimes bankruptcy, discredit, sorrow and bereavement. It sometimes causes heavy loss through friends, the knavery of others. It inevitably brings about a crisis in human affairs, causes great changes, dire straits, and in fact, the malice of fortune. You have to fear very great debility, lower vitality and rheumatism. To escape the loss through the bankruptcy of others, financial disaster, you will need to be either greatly circumspect in your dealings, or temporarily retire from money commitments in business. Avoid over-exertion.

Sun in good aspect to Mars.—This is an aspect which often coincides with marriage. It hardly ever fails to bring an offer of marriage.

Sun in good aspect to Neptune.—This aspect invariably brings advancement. One is enabled to improve one's position, increase one's business or stipend; but much will depend upon your own exertion. The aspect has been known in many cases to indicate a change for the better; sometimes it is a turning-point; a new road.

Sun in good aspect to Neptune.—This aspect often brings an offer of marriage; though it is at times attended with some difficulties and impediments.

Sun in good aspect to Uranus.—This aspect often coincides with beneficial changes and journeys. It brings business advancement or increase of stipend. It has been known to bring about an entire change in one's business mode of life, and is an aspect which often coincides with a turning. Sometimes it brings promotion, influential positions and power.

Sun in good aspect to Uranus.—This aspect sometimes brings an offer of marriage. It often coincides with a sudden marriage.

Sun in good aspect to Saturn.—This aspect imparts industry and a plodding spirit; consequently success attends strenuous efforts and industry. This aspect often brings gain in connection with business, property, land, agriculture, but especially in commerce connected with the earth's fruits. It often brings help or benefit from others.

Sun in good aspect to Saturn.—This aspect often brings marriage; sometimes marriage to an elderly man.

Sun in good aspect to the Moon.—This is a most propitious aspect for business; profit in trading. You should push your business for all it is worth. We have known many people make a lot of money under this aspect.

☉, ☌, ⚹, □, ⚼, ☍, or P. ♂. Inflammations, fevers, hurts, serious accidents, and often a violent death. In ♊ and ♐, inflammation of the lungs and a disordered nervous system, falls; in the watery signs, death by drowning; in ♍, danger of inflammation of the bowels; in the fixed signs, great liability to accidents; in ♌ or ♒ possible syncope, if the heart is weak. ♂ causes sudden events. The native under these directions is rashly inclined, rushing headlong into quarrels and disputes. A person with ♂ in the 2nd house during this direction, speculated rashly in business and soon became bankrupt. Amputations also are often necessary under this direction. It is more powerful if ♂ afflicted one or both of the luminaries at birth. It operates in the same way with females; they are likely to quarrel with their husbands. Child-birth is likely to be fatal. A person under this direction, burst a blood-vessel near the nose which resulted in death. A woman whose ☉ had progressed to ☌ and P. ♂ in the 5th house, died in child-birth, in spite of the best medical aid. It causes operations.

☉, ⩌, Sq., ✶, Q, △, or Bq., ♂. These bring physical activity and preferment, especially if in the army or navy; they incline to precipitancy in actions. The native will gain from those in whom ♂'s nature is dominant. Good for health and vitality; with females, offers of marriage and new friends.

☉, ☌, ⩌, Sq., ✶, Q, Bq., or P. ♀. Success in dealing in jewellery, apparel, and fancy goods; happiness and prosperity; love of amusement and pleasure. The principal aspects often cause marriage.

☉, ∠, or □ ♀. Trouble through females, children, and young persons; very unfavourable, causing great disappointments.

☉, ☌, ⩌, Sq., ✶, Q, or P. ☿. Public honours in literature, art or science, inventions, literary undertakings, etc., if the nativity portrays an aptitude for these things. This direction is sure to bring much mental activity and increase of business. Artists receive distinction under it. The editor of an influential London paper resigned his post, and started a very successful magazine of his own under this direction. A publisher and printer floated a paper under the same, many years ago, and is now reputed to be very wealthy.

☉, ∠, and □ ☿. Trouble through writings, disappointments in literature, publishing, etc.

☉ ☌ ☽. Success and new undertakings. If ☽ ☌ ☉ occurred at birth, the native is certain to receive much assistance, pecuniary and otherwise, from the other sex. The native may marry a very wealthy person. This direction frequently causes marriage in a male's natus.

☉, ⩌, Sq., ✶, Q, Bq., △, or P. ☽. A very good direction for business and finance; it often brings credit, preferment, and success in business. If the native is in the employment of others, he is sure to be promoted, or receive marks of favour from his employers and superiors. The △, P. and ☌ will bring marriage to either sex, especially if the ☉ and ☽ were in aspect at birth and dominant.

N.B.—The good aspect of the Sun to the Promittors ♂, ♄, ♅, ♆, ♀, ☿, and ♃, coincide with marriage if the subject is a woman and her horoscope does not deny marriage.

☉, ∠, □, ⚼, or ☍ ☽. Unfortunate for business and finance; speculation should be avoided: unfortunate for dealing with superiors and persons in power. When the ☉ or ☽ occupies the 6th house, serious indisposition may ensue. This direction sometimes causes heavy bereavement. With females it often brings a severe illness, especially if the ☽ squared or opposed the ☉ at birth, or either occupied the 6th house at birth, or by direction. Of course the strength of the aspect must be considered. Again, when the direction occurs from angles, aspects will be found to operate much more powerfully than in other parts of the horoscope. Aspects from angles and cardinal signs are the most powerful, producing the most marked results. Aspects are also more powerful from fixed signs than from common ones. In every case the radical horoscope must be considered carefully; for, when this indicates a strong, healthy, disease-resisting constitution, a bad direction may produce only a slight illness or temporary indisposition. On the other hand, a weak, debilitated constitution, as portrayed by the affliction of the luminaries at birth by ♄, may succumb to a direction which the more robust constitution would live through with ease. It is the same with regard to other affairs; for when the horoscope portrays loss and ill-fortune, a bad direction will bring more ill-fortune than in the case where good fortune is portrayed at birth.

Star Courses: Lunar Aspects to Promittors or Promissors.

☽, ☌, ∠, □, ⚼, ☍, or P. ♅. Very unfavourable. Unfortunate changes and journeys, mental anxiety and sometimes bereavement, odious notoriety when ♅ is dominant in the horoscope, suicide and intrigues with women when ♅ afflicted the ☽ at birth. With females, troubles and annoyances from males, changes and troublesome journeys.

☽, ⊻, Sq., ⚹, Q, Bq., or △, ♅. These are favourable, and, unless ♅ afflicted the ☽ at birth, may lead to a fortunate change and profitable journey, especially if ♅ or ☽ occupies the 3rd or 9th house by direction or at birth. Like the evil aspects, it also tends to attachments with females; it also brings unexpected good fortune.

☽, ☌, ∠, □, ⚼, ☍, or P. ♄. A very unfortunate direction. Losses, sorrows, disappointments, bereavements, serious illnesses, and to a weak constitution sometimes death. Generally, bereavement, grief, despondency, and fear of impending calamity, especially if ♄ afflicted the ☽ at birth. If ♄ or the ☽ occupies the 2nd house, bankruptcy is to be feared.

☽, ⊻, Sq., ⚹, Q, Bq., or △, ♄. Success; the accumulation of wealth by personal industry; the native manages his affairs with tact and precision.

☽, ☌, ⊻, Sq., ⚹, Q, Bq., △, or P. ♃. Exceptional success in business, preferment, and the increase of wealth; it also often brings marriage; with females it gives success, good health, new friends, and benefits from those in whom ♃'s nature is dominant.

☽, ∠, □, ⚼, or ☍ ♃. These aspects cause extravagance and losses in business. It is an unfortunate time for litigation; judges are sure to go against the native. With females it causes indisposition through irregular circulation and rush of blood to the head, particularly if the direction occur from cardinal signs.

☽, ☌, ∠, □, ⚼, ☍, or P. ♂. These directions are remarkable for causing accidents, hurts, inflammatory diseases, and fevers. When under this aspect, especially if ♂ afflicted the ☽ at birth, the native is irritable, indiscreet, and quarrelsome; he may experience bladder and kidney troubles, especially if ♂ occupies the 6th house. Persons under this direction should avoid disputes and dangerous places; they may lose by fire or theft. With females it acts the same as with males. Every person whose ☽ was afflicted at birth by ♂, is liable, when under this direction, to death by violence, fever, or inflammation. A female in child-birth would be in imminent danger of death, especially if ♂ occupies the 5th house.

☽, ⚺, Sq., ✶, Q, Bq., or △, ♂. These bring physical activity, increase of business, and often very successful journeys. The native is courageous, self-confident, and adventuresome. This direction increases the disease-resisting faculties. It is the same with a female who, if ♂ occupies the 5th house, is likely to form an attachment which may lead to trouble, especially if there are other indications of this in the nativity.

☽, ☌, ⚺, Sq., ✶, Q, Bq., △, or P. ☉. Help from friends. The P. and ☌ cause marriage; the ☌ brings changes and new enterprises, much help from powerful and wealthy females if ☽ ☌ ☉ occurred at birth. The native may marry a wealthy person under this direction, especially if ☽ ☌ ☉ occurred at birth and near the 7th or 8th house. These aspects bring success in business, promotion, and general prosperity. The ☽ ☌ ☉ often causes indisposition, specially if they were in ☌, □ or ☍ at birth, and either occupies the 6th house.

☽, ∠, □, ⚼, or ☍, ☉. Unfortunate for native's affairs; bad for speculation; losses and annoyances are plentiful; danger of bereavement and ill-health, particularly in the case of a female. From angles, and especially from cardinal signs, this aspect is very powerful. The native should not push his affairs.

☽, ☌, ⚺, Sq., ✶, Q, Bq., △, or P. ♀. Love of pleasure and success therein. Merchants, jewellers, dealers in male and female attire, will be very prosperous. It points strongly to an increase of offspring, particularly when ♀ or the ☽ occupies the 5th house and children are not denied.

☽, ∠, □, ⚼, or ☍, ♀. Unfortunate; trouble, annoyances, and disappointments from females; sometimes bereavement. With females it causes temporary indisposition and a disordered system.

☽, ☌, ⚺, Sq., ✶, Q, Bq., △, or P. ☿. Mental activity, study, and, if the natus portrays it, success in literature, science, or art. It may also bring a lawsuit or dealings with lawyers and literary men; fortunate for writings, agreements, publishing, and applications for secretariships.

☽, ∠, □, ⚼, or ☍, ☿. Unfortunate for writings, law, agreements, and literary undertakings; difficulty in passing examinations, etc.

☽, ☌, P., ⚺, Sq., ✶, or △ to her own place at birth, brings success, journeys (especially if the ☽ occupied the 3rd, 9th, or 12th house), and new friends of both sexes.

☽, ∠, □, ⚼, or ☍, ☽ radix. Unfortunate; annoyances through females, slight temporary indisposition.

Moon in good aspect to Neptune.—This often brings slight gain by journeys, also money or business gain.

Moon in good aspect to Uranus.—This inclines to journeys; profitable journeys; a little gain in business. Sometimes it coincides with courtship in the horoscope of a man.

Moon in adverse aspect to Neptune.—Sometimes causes a cold, a little indisposition, conflicts; loss in connection with changes, journeys and money ventures.

Moon in adverse aspect to Uranus.—Also unfavourable for changes and journeys. It often causes much mental anxiety; sometimes a cold, indisposition, annoyance from the other sex.

Star Courses: Directions of the Planets: Promittors or Promissors.

♅, □, ☍, P., or ☌, ♄. These are powerful when ♅ and ♄ are dominant in the figure. In the 7th, unhappiness in marriage, and a very bad marriage partner; in the 10th, unpopularity and disagreeable rumours.

♅, Sq., ✶, or △, ♄. Undesirable, though they tend to stability and power.

♅, ☌, P., Sq., ✶, or △, ♃. These often bring money or legacies.

♅, ∠, ⚼, □, or ☍, ♃. Bad for litigation, loss of money.

♅, ✶, or △, ♂. Success in antagonisms, if ♂ be dominant and well-aspected.

♅, ∠, ⚼, □, ☍, P., or ☌, ♂. Unfortunate. In the 10th, unpopularity, quarrels, troubles in business; in the 7th, worries, antagonisms, quarrels with the marriage partner; in the 12th, active secret foes and danger of imprisonment. A man with ♂ in the 12th ☍ ♅ suffered imprisonment when the ☽ by progressive motion reached the □ of ♂ and ♅.

♅ *in evil aspect to* ♀. Trouble through the other sex; sometimes a liaison or scandal. Females under this direction should be very careful in their dealings with males.

♅ *in good aspect to* ♀. A strong love of the other sex is likely to result.

♅ *afflicting* ☿. Often causes newspaper controversy; trouble through writings, great inclination for occult studies; the mind is wayward, sarcastic, and uncertain; reverses in literature, opposition and hostility in various ways are likely.

♅ *in good aspect to* ☿. Strong inclination for study, especially of science, human nature, occultism, astrology, phrenology, etc. The native gains much by observation and practical experience, is inclined to originality of thought and indifference to creeds; it also gives tact and precision.

♄, ☌, P. *or in good aspect to* ♃. Often brings inheritance, legacies, etc.; also successful lawsuits, honours, popularity, and church preferment.

♄ *afflicting* ♃. Unfortunate for law and litigation. The native will experience losses and obstacles in various ways, unsuccessful investments, and loss by bank failures.

♄ *in good aspect to* ♂. Gives courage, firmness, stability.

♄ *in evil aspect to* ♂. Great malice and violence. If ♂ or ♄ occupies the 1st, 10th, 3rd or 9th house, the native may commit a crime (perhaps murder), may meet with a serious accident, be maimed, hanged, or imprisoned. An acquaintance who had ♂ □ ♄, from 10th and 1st houses, met with a serious accident, when this aspect became complete, and was crippled for life; in this instance ♂ afflicted the ☽ at birth.

♄ *afflicting* ♀. Trouble through the other sex. This direction is disastrous for courtship, and often causes grief and bereavement; also disreputable habits and frequent scandal; certainly disappointment.

♄ *in good aspect to* ♀. This inclines to reserve, modesty, and good conduct; also to constancy in attachment.

♄ *afflicting* ☿. The temper is very captious. The native is liable to pilfer, or take part in illicit transactions, which may bring him into trouble; especially if ☿ and ♄ are dominant in the horoscope and ☿ be afflicted at birth. Good aspects of ♃ and ♀ at birth counteract the tendency to fraud and knavery.

♄ *in good direction to* ☿. The person will be careful, reserved, serious, thoughtful, cautious. There will be tact in managing affairs.

♃ *ill-aspected by* ♂. The native is vain and adventuresome, hasty, extravagant, and reckless. It is bad for lawsuits and contention. In the 2nd or 8th house it causes great extravagance.

♃ *in good aspect to* ♂. Promotion, honour, much success. If ♃ is in the 2nd, pecuniary success. A person with ♃ in the 5th house under this direction won a large sum in turf speculation.

♃ *in bad aspect to* ♀. Pride, great extravagance in dress, ornaments, amusements.

♃ *in good aspect to* ♀. Social success, and in dealings with females.

♃ ☌, P. *or in good aspect with* ☿. Credit and distinction in literature or public speaking, and gain therefrom. This aspect elevates the mind, makes the native prudent and sincere, and inspires successful plans.

♃ *afflicting* ☿. Mental trouble, wrong notions in general. An acquaintance with ☿ ☍ ♃ from 1st and 7th houses suffered mental derangement, and had much trouble in his transactions, this position being very bad for litigation, and portraying heavy losses. Litigants generally have the ☉ and ☿ afflicted by ♃ either at birth or by direction.

♂ *afflicting* ♀. Flirtation and sometimes scandal. If either or both are in the 7th, domestic quarrels will take place. When ♂ occupies the 5th in the case of a female, trouble and misfortune through the other sex are portrayed.

♂ *in good aspect to* ♀. Extravagance, love of pleasure and the other sex; it often brings females to grief.

♂ *afflicting* ☿. The temper is short; the native may commit a theft if ☿ was afflicted at birth; danger of quarrels, disputes, or (if the nativity denotes it) lawsuits.

♂ *in good aspect to* ☿. Mental energy; the mind is quick, sharp, and penetrating; the native is precise, and often obtains distinction in mechanical science or engineering.

♀ P. *or in good aspect to* ☿. Very good; distinction in poetry, music, or art, if the nativity shows ability for these things; the native is merry, witty, laughter-loving, and susceptible to poetical inspiration. A friend with ♀ in the 9th at birth, P. to ☿, obtained more than local distinction in poetry and music under this direction.

In all forecasts great attention must be paid to the radical horoscope. It would be absurd to predict literary distinction, poetical inspiration, exceptional pecuniary success, or any other incident of life, unless these things are portrayed in the nativity, *i.e.*, promised by Promittors in the horoscope.

CHAPTER XIX.

As an example of how to read the horoscope, we reprint the test horoscope which appeared in *Borderland* and *Pearson's Weekly*.

Only the birth-data were given, and about half a dozen astrologers and students accepted the test. But this horoscope alone vindicated astrology.

THE "REVIEW OF REVIEWS" AND ASTROLOGY.

Mr. Stead made the following announcement in the *Review of Reviews* of February 15th, 1893, page 181:

AN EXPERIMENT IN HOROSCOPES.

So much has been written of late as to the ability of astrologers to delineate character and predict the probable course of life, that I have consented to a suggestion which was made me by a Yorkshire astrologer to submit the claims of the professors of this science to a somewhat crucial test. He suggests that five other students of astrology shall consent to take part in this experiment. I will make a selection of half a dozen persons who are able to state the exact time of their birth within fifteen minutes. I will send the birth moment of each of these six persons to each of these six astrologers, mentioning the latitude and longitude of the place where they were born, and the sex. No other particulars will be given them. They will then be required to work out according to their own method all that they can tell of the character, past history, and future prospects of each of the half a dozen subjects. Each person whose birth moment is submitted to the astrologers will be requested to draw up a statement, and forward it to me in a sealed envelope, filling in briefly a return under the following heads:

1. The qualities of the mind and disposition.
2. Health, susceptibility to disease, liability to accidents, etc.
3. Pecuniary prospects.
4. Ability or aptitude for business, and success, or otherwise.
5. Happy, or otherwise, if married.
6. Children.
7. Travels through life.
8. Probable benefit by friends or persecution from foes.
9. The good and ill periods of life, the time when sickness, accidents, bereavement, loss or acquisition of a fortune, the loss of credit or business and new enterprises.

These envelopes will be kept in my possession until I receive the horoscopes from the astrologers; they will then be opened, and their contents compared with the conclusions which have been arrived at by the astrologers. The chances of the astrologers being able to hit off the features of all the six cases submitted to them are not very great, and nobody can be surprised if the experiment results in a total failure. On the other hand, if it should succeed, even in half the cases, it will be very remarkable, and will require to be explained by something other than the long arm of coincidence.

An Astrological Curiosity.

(From *Pearson's Weekly*.)

I wonder if my readers will think me too egotistical in publishing the matter that occupies this page? It is printed exactly as it appeared in Mr. W. T. Stead's *Borderland*. Mr. Stead's introduction to the horoscope explains it thoroughly, and there is no need for me to add anything further. I am not in the least a believer in occult science, but, at the same time, so many points in this horoscope are so curiously accurate, that I thought almost anybody would probably be interested in glancing through it. I do not think there is the least doubt about the fact that Mr. Wilde had not the smallest knowledge of the personality of the individual whose horoscope he was casting. In my notes I have only referred to the points on which I can safely speak. No man is a reliable judge of his own character.

Extract from *Review of Reviews*, May, 1900.

HIS CHARACTER WRITTEN IN THE STARS.

I have never written a character sketch in which I have had such ample material for describing the character of its subject, for in Mr. Pearson's case I have the advantage of a minute analysis of his character drawn up by an astrologer who knew nothing about him, not even his name, and that analysis has been checked by Mr. Pearson himself. We have therefore his character as the stars, according to the science of astrology, say it ought to be, and we have Mr. Pearson's own testimony as to how far the astrologer has correctly delineated his mental, moral, and social characteristics. The material was obtained in this wise. When I was publishing *Borderland*, I thought it would be a good experiment to get the birth date of some person whose name was familiar to the public, but the details of whose history and character were not generally familiar or easily accessible. The range of choice was somewhat limited, for most people whose names are well known have their biographies more or less written at large in the "Men of the Time," and the mention of their birthday is often sufficient to give a clue to their identity. This, however, was not the case with Mr. Pearson. He happened to know the moment of his birth, and it may safely be said that there was a very remote possibility that the astrologer to whom I sent the horoscope would have ascertained the person to whom that birthday's date belonged. Mr. Pearson certainly did not communicate with the astrologer, for he was much interested in the experiment himself, nor did I think Mr. George Wilde, the astrologer in question, whose address is 6, Central Street, Halifax, would take any pains to ascertain from the Parish Register or otherwise who the person was whose horoscope he was drawing. Mr. Wilde took a great deal of trouble with the horoscope of his subject, and after spending much time and devoting much labour to its elaboration, he sent me the following statement of what, by the rules of astrological science, ought to be the characteristics of a person born at Wookey, near Wells, 11 a.m., February 24th, 1866.

A TEST NATIVITY.—MR. PEARSON, OF *PEARSON'S WEEKLY*.

BY MR. GEORGE WILDE.

Some years ago, before *Borderland* was started, the claims of astrologers led me to propose a test of the science, which, unfortunately, was never carried out. I suggested that half a dozen astrologers should be invited to cast the horoscopes of some half a dozen persons, of whom they were to know nothing except their sex and the place and moment of their birth. The proposal fell through for two reasons. First, there were not half a dozen astrologers to be found who were willing to undertake the test. Secondly, I could not get the birth dates of half a dozen persons notable enough to be interesting, but not notable enough to be identified by the place and date of their birth. Ultimately the test dwindled down to one horoscope cast by one astrologer. His success, however, was so remarkable as to arrest attention. The subject whose birth-moment was selected for the test was Mr. Pearson, of *Pearson's Weekly*—a name familiar everywhere

—although no reference library or biographical dictionary enables the astrologer to use his birth date as a key to his identity. The astrologer who cast the horoscope was Mr. George Wilde, Halifax, Yorkshire. I print the horoscope as it was written, with Mr. Pearson's notes and comments.

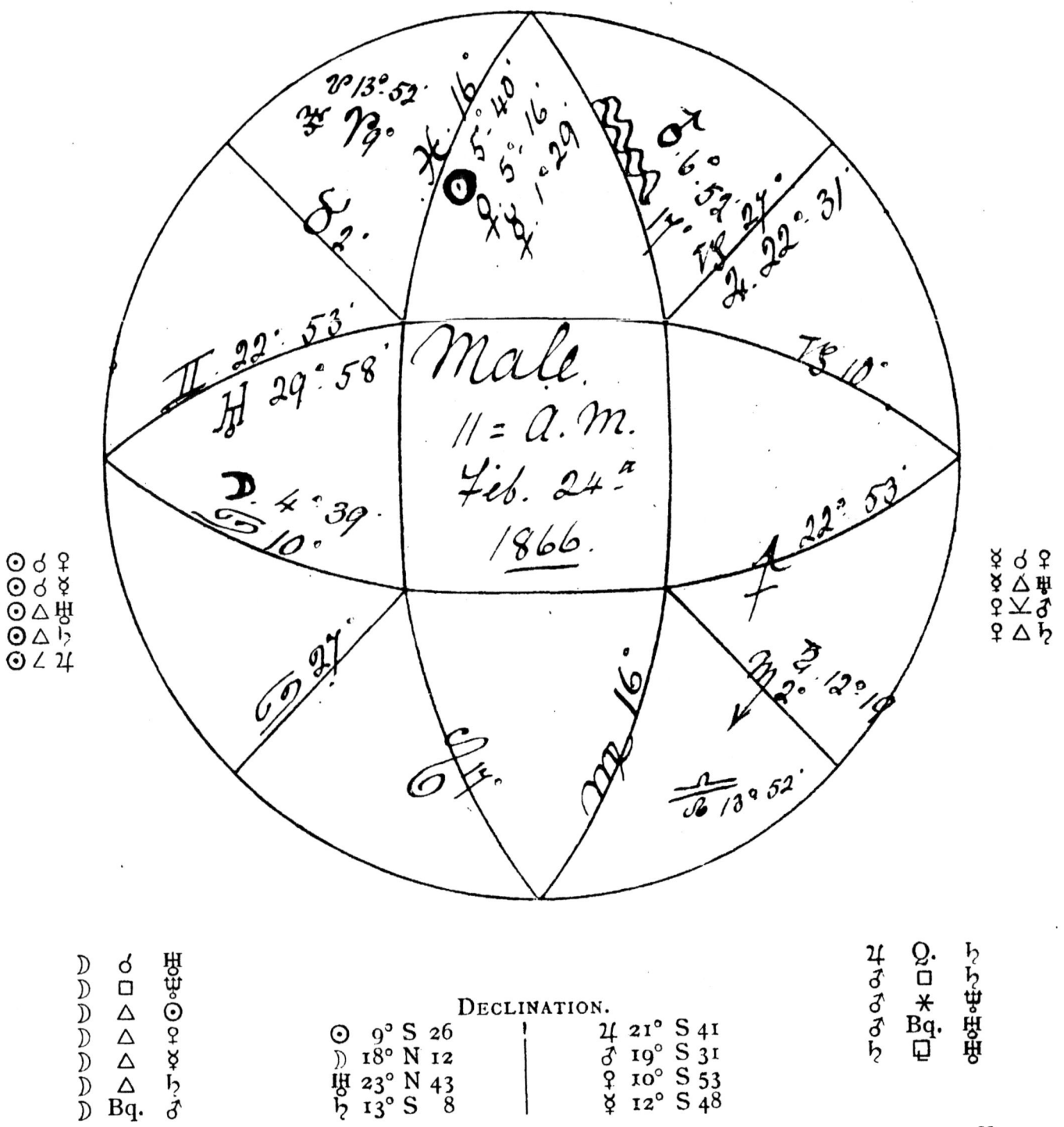

Male.
11 = a.m.
Feb. 24.
1866.

DECLINATION.

☉ 9° S 26 ♃ 21° S 41
☽ 18° N 12 ♂ 19° S 31
♅ 23° N 43 ♀ 10° S 53
♄ 13° S 8 ☿ 12° S 48

HOROSCOPE OF A MALE BORN FEBRUARY 24TH, 1866, 11 A.M.

Computed for Wookey, near Wells.

☿ △ ♅
♀ △ ♄
♀ ☌ ☿
♀ △ ♅
♂ □ ♄
☽ △ ☿
☽ △ ♀

I.—MENTAL QUALITIES AND DISPOSITION.

1.—A quick, active, generous person, studious, contemplative, highly ingenious, and inventive; possessing finesse, originality of thought, rapid sequence of ideas. Penetrating, opinionative, independent, candid, truthful, proud, slightly eccentric, sociable, pleasing, courteous, judicious, kind-hearted, in fact, excessively good-natured; much appreciated and respected by others, versatile in mind, lacking tenacity of purpose.

2.—He is constant in attachment, delighting in close friendship, possessing warmth of affection and sensuousness almost reaching the amorous spirit.

3.—The honour, candour, and rectitude of the man are exceptional, and his word is as good as his bond; fond of company, agreeable, delighting in oratory, languages, music, and art; for he has musical, literary, and artistic ability or talent, a keen appreciation of the beautiful in art, form, and nature.

♂ *in the 9th*

4.—He has special aptitude for acquiring languages, is comprehensive, eloquent, highly impressionable, an observer, critical and quick to detect inconsistencies in others. (5) Self-willed, almost headstrong, obstinate and almost jealous; would be severe with evil-doers (6).

♂ □ ♄ and ♅ *in the asc.*

His obstinacy and severity are, however, obscured ingredients, certainly not to the fore. This combination begets force of character, executive and propelling power, an iron hand hidden beneath the velvet glove. The temper is even, and certainly not captious even under provocation, and the disposition is genial, merry, witty, fond

♀ ☌ ☿ *and in the 10th*

of sport (7), and society (8), singing, dancing (9), and the stage. (10) The nativity bears the impress of a genius, indicating imagination and inspiration with tremendous impulse.

MR. PEARSON'S NOTES AND COMMENTS.

1.—I cannot pretend to be a judge of all this. Those who know me well say it is pretty true.

2.—I think this right.

3.—Not that I know of. I am very good on tunes, but detest music. I like a landscape by Leader, but I can see nothing to admire in an old master.

4.—This I doubt, but I have never tried beyond acquiring enough French to make myself understood.

5.—Yes.

6.—No, I always try not to be rough on people.

7.—Very.

8.—Loathe society in the ordinary acceptation of the term. I thoroughly enjoy being with a few friends, and my real friends are very few.

9.—Very.

10.—Moderately.

☽ △ ☿ and ♀	11.—He is rather mutable in mind, chiefly through rapid sequence of ideas, and has a subtle fancy, sagacity, and incisive wit.	11.—Good.
☽ △ ♄	12.—The horoscope indicates that he is on the best of terms with himself, though reverses would tend to make him, at times, disconsolate and reserved. He has an eye to his own interests, and possesses tact and diplomacy.	12.—Good.
☽ in ♋ △ ♀ ☿ ☌ ♀	The temperament inclines rather to the feminine principles than to the masculine, and there is much tenderness, much fine metal in the composition; he is fine-grained, gentle, obliging, neat in dress, precise. frugal and has few extremes, well conducted and orderly. He has a horror of anything low, coarse or vulgar, has tender susceptibilities, is ambitious of honour, his *amour propre* is easily wounded, censure or praise exercises an undoubted influence over him. (13) He has considerable will-power	
♂ in 9th	and self-assertion; the combination of these ingredients generate an impulsive, headstrong spirit; but he is well-meaning in spirit and well-intentioned. He has special aptitude for acquiring a large amount of intellectual culture. and is fond of change and travel (14).	13.—Yes. 14.—Good.
☽ △ ♄	He dislikes the rowdy element in others (15), and down in the utmost recesses of his being a spice of timidity (16) and caution are to be found, which restrain him a good deal. There is no aggressiveness. waspishness. or irritability in the composition; the amiable qualities are to the fore.	15.—Yes. 16.—I'm shy at the bottom.
☽ △ ☿ ☽ △ ♄ ☽ △ ♀ ♃ in 9th	17.—He is rapid and accurate in his perceptions and mental operations, and is, perhaps, sensitively highly-strung, and his vivacity is tempered with a spice of sadness.	17.—Doctors always tell me my nerves are exceptionally high-strung.
	He is by no means positive or dogmatic, though he has well-defined principles and is conscientious; his motives are pure and sincere.	
No aspect of ♂ to ☉ or ☿	He would do with more propelling power, and, whatever his mission. he is not inspired, enthusiastic, or terribly in earnest.	
	18.—He is not easily elated or depressed.	18.—Not true.
♂ in 9th	19.—I do not think spirituality has a marked place in his composition, or that he would worship his Divine Maker through	19.—Good.

fear of the unknown. Doubtless his religious convictions clash with those of sectarians and creedists, and he has considerable moral courage; but I do not think his faith is great, as there are indications of some scepticism in the composition.

He may pray, but I am not sure that he believes—at least, not implicitly.

☽ △ ♀ & ☿ ☌ ♀

20.—His sympathy is with the multitude and with the young and helpless.

20.—*Vide* Fresh Air Fund.

☽ △ ☿ △ ♄
☿ ☌ ♀ ♂ □ ♄
and ♂ in 9th
♃ in 9th
♀ ☌ ☉
☿ ☌ ☉

He is philanthropic but not prodigal; he is ardent, but lacks vehemence, is discreet and circumspect. The reasoning powers are not specially marked, but deductive judgment is here marked. He is emotional and has great depth of feeling, which impresses and influences him much. The mind is analytical, and he has larger perspicuity, and is, perhaps, more a windbag than a thinker; (21) his speech is more pathetic than forcible. He has genuine wit, and can, perhaps, be facetious or humorous. He is not particularly a demonstrative man (22), and would do with more determination and a stronger personality. He has many of those noble qualities which command the respect and esteem of others. He is a man who will meet with a great deal of good fortune (23), has tremendous ambition, and is fond of curiosities; occult subjects have some attraction for him (24).

21. I fancy this is so.

22.—Right.

23.—Right so far.

24.—Right.

HEALTH.

☉ ☌ ♀

♂ □ ♄
and ♄ in 6th

A strong constitution, a disease-resisting temperament, and fairly good health are portrayed; slight organic weakness of the active system and heart—probably bladder troubles; gravel or stone, throat troubles and an indifferent state of the liver and blood. These things, however, are only to be expected later on in life. He is liable to accidents, serious hurts, and should be careful during journeys and on the water: he is liable to hurts to the legs and ankles (25).

25.—Very true

☽ △ ♀
☽ △ ☿
☽ △ ☉

PECUNIARY PROSPECTS.

Considerable financial success and lucrative positions are indicated; prosperity, the accumulation of money, and the acquisition of estate and riches.

☽ △ ☿ △ ♀
♀ ☌ ☿
and ♀ and ☿
on the M.C.

EMPLOYMENT OR PROFESSION.

The horoscope portrays literary employment or employment in connection with poetry, music, the stage, wines, and as a stationer, printer, bookseller, schoolmaster, publisher, and journalist (26). The natus is suggestive of employment, at some time in life, in connection with liquids, chemistry, or occult science; he has special aptitude for the study of astrology, though he may not know it. The horoscope portrays promotion, preferment, help from persons in power (27); he is certain to be highly esteemed by his superiors. Positions of trust are in store for him, honours, etc. He has special aptitude for business, and will succeed as a merchant.

26.—Curiously accurate if, as I suppose, the first indicated is the most probable.

27.—Never very bad.

☽ △ ♀
☽ △ ☉

MARRIAGE.

☽ □ ♆ and ☽ ☌ ♅ often cause trouble in the married life, which he appears to have had since. A happy marriage and domestic felicity; the wife will be of high social status, independent, high-minded, accomplished, refined, constant in attachment, generous, noble-hearted, straightforward. Trouble, however, from females is indicated, if he is not circumspect (28).

28.—Good to last paragraph, which has not come to pass yet.

CHILDREN.

Offspring are portrayed, though this question can only be accurately deduced from the horoscopes of husband and wife (29).

29.—Three girls.

TRAVELLING.

♂ in 9th

Many journeys are portrayed (30), and Mars' position threatens dangers; changes of a sudden nature are indicated, which do not all conduce to good fortune.

30.—Good.

□ ♄, and ☽ in the 1st house

FRIENDS.

♄ in 6th

Many powerful friends are portrayed, ☉ ☌ ☿ and ♀; and trouble or annoyance from servants or inferiors (31).

31.—Have so far had exceptionally little trouble of this kind.

HONOUR.

☉ ♀ and ☿ in the 10th

A more than local fame and distinction are indicated, and he is destined to be much in evidence, much before the public at some period of life.

II.—LIFE'S HISTORY.

Directions, or stars in their courses:—
The third year of life was a critical year for health; throat troubles (32) and feverish complaints were indicated, some liability to hurts, drowning, accidents, and falls (33).

A chill would emanate from a journey. The liability to accidents would continue up to his seventh year, when Mars would complete his quartile aspect with Saturn.

At five, he would display special and marked aptitude for learning, and would acquire knowledge very quickly. The seventh year portrayed changes, indisposition, and probably a chill. He would make rapid progress in his studies, particularly in music (34), art, and literature, and would gain by friends, as Mercury and Venus were in company during the early years of life.

At school, in the race of learning he would leave most of his compeers behind, and should acquire honours, distinction, and scholarships with little effort (35).

The tenth year was an unfortunate one for health, and again chills, throat troubles and accidents were to be feared; the credit would fluctuate. He may have experienced bereavement in the family (36), probably an aunt or uncle would know him no more, and unfavourable journeys would result; still he would most probably gain by wills; from the dead and from friends (37).

The twelfth, thirteenth, and fourteenth, and possibly fifteenth years indicated legacies, help from a powerful friend, exceptional success in his studies, credit, help from kindred. His genius and imagination would begin to assert themselves.

The thirteenth and fourteenth years portray slight indisposition (38), bereavement, changes of an undesirable nature, and probable trouble and annoyance from the other sex. The fifteenth and sixteenth years portray beneficial journeys, gain by science, friends, literature, theology, and preferment; he would most probably commence business, or go to college, or enter some profession (39).

These years were successful ones, and

32.—Right.

33.—Most children of three fall about a good deal.

34.—Never even learned my notes.

35.—I got a good many prizes at school; never tried for a scholarship.

36.—Uncle died when I was twelve.

37.—Never was left a penny.

38.—Had a very severe attack of scarlet fever.

39.—Decided not to take Holy Orders—an idea with which I had been brought up.

would bring credit and honours. The seventeenth (1883) prefigured indisposition, and probably trouble with the throat; again falls and hurts (40) were indicated; annoyance through creedists, or the other sex; new literary friends, and assistance therefrom (41).

The eighteenth year indicated friction, annoyance, slight indisposition, hurts in sports (42), and a tendency to act precipitantly; loss of relatives (43), disputes with those in power, and sudden changes were imminent.

The nineteenth and twentieth years were indicative of honours, advancement (44), assistance from friends, new enterprises, success in literature, art, or music; new friends, success at social functions; the stars would strongly incline him to the company of the other sex, and to marriage (45). The probability is he would be much in evidence and much before the public at this time; he would achieve distinction in music, art, or literature; some literary and powerful friend would assist him.

He would gain by long journeys, religion, or science. A female friend might cause him annoyance, probably through some indiscretion (46).

In the twenty-first and twenty-second years friends of both sexes would do a great deal for his good and ill; one friend would assist him much, whilst another would prove adverse. Some lady would be much in evidence in this part of his life, and would undoubtedly influence and assist him much (47).

The twenty-first year portrayed changes, journeys, help from powerful friends, preferment; gain by literature, music, or science.

The twenty-second and twenty-third years portray marriage or great inclination for the society of the other sex; pleasure, music, literature, and art.

He would acquire preferment and distinction at this time, new enterprises and beneficial changes are indicated (48).

He would be much in evidence, much in harness, and very much to the fore in things in which he was connected, and much before the public; gain in business and financial success accompanied by a

40.—Had two very bad falls off bicycles, one of which injured me badly.

41.—Very serious attack of calf love.

42.—Was badly hit on the head playing hockey.

43.—Lost an uncle.

44.—Got on very well and rapidly in business.

45.—Got engaged.

46.—Wrong.

47.—Got married.

48.—Started *Pearson's Weekly* at twenty-four, and was immediately very successful.

high expenditure. The latter part of the twenty-third year, however, indicated some indisposition, loss and trouble from servants, possibly bereavement, a chill, and throat or bladder troubles (49).

The twenty-fourth year would bring disasters, sudden loss, discredit and imposition by or through friends; anxiety, accusations, indisposition, loss and annoyance by or through servants, workmen, and inferiors; loss by or through journeys, quarrels, or disputes, probably with publishers and friends (50).

Things were done secretly and unknown to him, which were detrimental to his interests, as he afterwards found out to his cost; credit and discredit would result, and there was some liability to accidents; cross influences were at work throughout the year, but the bad fortune met with was decidedly in excess of the good.

The early months of the twenty-fifth year would bring annoyance, unfavourable influences, and possibly slight loss. The summer and closing months would bring increase of business, pecuniary success, and better fortune; activity, journeys, gain by wills and from friends of both sexes, and if not already married the influences would tempt him to marry this year. He would still feel very much the evil effects of the previous year's bad influences, and the probability is he would feel the effects for a year or two, as a direction of this kind has been known to cripple a man for several years.

He would gain a great deal from a powerful friend of the other sex this year, and be brought prominently before the public.

The twenty-sixth year portrayed mental activity, literary undertakings, or new enterprises; he would be very much in harness and would gain from literary friends (51).

Twenty-seventh year, 1893; changes, or a desire for changes and journeys, slight loss or annoyance, some anxiety and worry, much mental and physical activity, gain by science, and during the middle or latter part of the year he might be brought very prominently before the public.

GEO. WILDE.

49.—Wrong.

50.—Left George Newnes. Rest all wrong, as this was my first year in business for myself, the foundation of whatever prosperity I have had.

51.—" Missing Word.'

C. A. PEARSON.

CHAPTER XX.

STAR COURSE EXPERIENCES.

FERDINAND MAXIMILIAN, Emperor of Mexico, was born at 4 a.m., July 6th, 1832, Vienna. The horoscope affords a striking example of the truth of the ancient system of directing. At birth ☉ is □ ♂. On June 19th, 1867, the day of his death, the Sun was □ ♂ and P. The ☽ was also opposed to ♂. Mars was in the 11th house, the ☉ was in the 2nd house, and he was betrayed into the hands of the Republican leader, Juarez. Followers of Ptolemy ignore the influences of the houses in nativities and directions, observing only the angles as sources of power; they have assumed that the other houses are influential only in Horary Astrology.

By pretended friendship, the emperor was lured to his destruction and shot! ♂ in the 11th house was the snare.

Before testimony is presented to the public in support of a much derided science, it should be submitted to the scrutiny of responsible people. The letters of testimony of our forecasts in the case of Mr. L——, a private gentleman, have been submitted to, and inspected by the publishers, Messrs. Foulsham & Co. This should always be the case, for the student should have confidence in the asserted predictions. The horoscope was cast, and the foreknowledge given, many years ago; we append the horoscope, the map showing the positions at the thirty-second birthday, and another displaying the positions at the thirty-fourth birthday.

Our object is not only to demonstrate the truth of the directions, but to prove beyond doubt the potency of the influences of the houses, coincident with the courses of the stars and their aspects with each other. It will be observed that in the native's thirty-first year, the Sun came to a quartile aspect of Neptune, and at the same time within orb □ ♄. Neptune is in the 9th house, the Sun is in the 11th, and Saturn is in the 3rd house. We should expect that evil would come from friends and through journeys principally, also through relatives; and that from the radical positions of

☽ ☌ ♂ in the 9th house and ☽ ☍ ♄, there would be aggressive fortune, as well as danger attending journeys.

The ☉ also is P. ♅. The extraordinary thing about these directions is, that during a good lunar direction, he was tempted to embark in promising things, or induced to travel to his detriment and loss.

For instance, ☽ ☌ ☉ at the end of 1895, and ☽ △ ♄ at the beginning of 1896, were snares; for they sent him to Paris on a misrepresentation, and then the solar aspects immediately began to exert their power; though he had not previously felt their hostility.

The Moon was a kind of red-herring, or bait, to lure him into the hands of the powerful solar enemies. Certainly the Moon was a decoy, for until she formed a good aspect with Saturn and the Sun, he received no overtures. But here are extracts from his letter side by side with our forecasts:

Prognostications.	Mr. L———'s Remarks.
1.—☽ ☌ ☉ and ☽△♄ coincide with the closing months of 1895 and the opening months of 1896. Both are favourable aspects; one indicating enterprises, business gain, or offers from friends.	1.—"About the early part and middle of 1896, I did have offers from friends. But they were all of a doubtful character, as events proved, and calculated to bring no benefit."
2.—Slight gain from journeys or people at a distance.	2.—"A journey to Paris for a month in 1896 brought a present of money from a friend from India; much against my wish."
3.—You will have a great desire to change and remove. You have been very unsettled for ☉ P. ♅ still obtains.	3.—"All 1895 and half of 1896 I had a great desire to change and remove. But all seemed the result of pressing, adverse circumstances."
4.—A friend may mislead you and cause you trouble.	4.—"In the middle of 1896 a friend—close relation—did mislead me terribly, causing me to leave England at the end of July on a wild-goose chase; loss of all my capital on a worthless enterprise and empty promises. Also caused a serious breach of friendship with my mother, and a final stranding in Paris with my wife and child without hope or a friend. This trouble was most severe; for the author of it had had my confidence all my life."
5.—These remarks especially apply to January, February, and March, 1897, when ☽ ☌ ☿, ☽ ✶ ♂, ☽ ☌ ♅, come up. ☽ ☌ ☿ is sure to bring much mental activity, writing, and probably literary work. ☽ ☌ ♅ is sure to project much evil.	5.—"These were very adverse months. Much mental activity and a little study also. I wrote a little."

6.—Loss and trouble through a friend about the middle of 1897 may be expected.

7.—Still the Spring of 1897 will bring some gain.

8.—You may expect annoyance August 27th to September 3rd.

9.—October 8th to 17th you will feel an adverse influence, much annoyance, $\odot \square \psi$, $\odot$ P. H, $\odot \square \hbar$ all operating with evil mien.

6.—"This came true, although I had used every care; but it was through my landlord."

7.—"My wife had a legacy of 900 francs; but the lawyer swindled her out of all but 200 francs."

8.—"Great trouble and annoyance came all along these months.

9.—"Very true. I had to leave my abode in Paris on my return to England in the early morning, 5 a.m., of the 8th, having to regularly fight my way out from the building with the aid of hired men and police. The landlord tried to stop my furniture on an illegal plea for repairs,

Mr. L——'s Remarks.

my men were knocked down and my wife assaulted.

" My experience would have turned many brains.

" I was in some danger, for I was present at the Bazaar de la Charité fire, expecting my sister to be there, who was prevented from attending by a fortunate circumstance. I was at the time bad friends with her, therefore imagine my state of mind with all those dreadful sights, whilst searching amongst the charred remains.

" My experiences do strike me as having been somewhat more than usually falls to the lot of man. In my remarks I forgot to refer to a letter you wrote me from Germany, November 30th, 1896, in which you tell me I should not have gone abroad, saying, That I am threatened in health and fortune, by indignities, litigation, sorrow, and heavy loss.

" How very true all this proved, you have my letters to say. You warned me specially against April 1st, 2nd, 11th, and 12th, 1897. The very dates I went to my new quarters in Paris, Rue Brunel, Boulevard Peirere, which resulted in litigation. Indignities were plentiful, and I had to conduct my case in court without a lawyer. You say 1898 will also be adverse, and this is true enough so far. You have warned me against going abroad, because of the conjunction of the Moon and Mars in my 9th house and the opposition of the ☽ to ♄ in the 3rd house. Your prophecies have been verified again and again. You say in the horoscope—journeys will be attended with dangers and ill-fortune; do not go abroad, for you are in immediate danger of accidents and of ill-health, as well as loss.

" I nearly lost my sight and my life by a laboratory accident in India in 1891. I also had some unusual and uncomfortable experiences during my voyages, and have always been liable to hurts to my head. I was once thrown over a bridge on to the crown of my head, a bed of nettles at the edge of the brook broke my fall. Even short journeys are dangerous for me; for during my schooldays, big boys and men have been aggressively brutal in their handling of me, with a sort of thoughtless enmity."

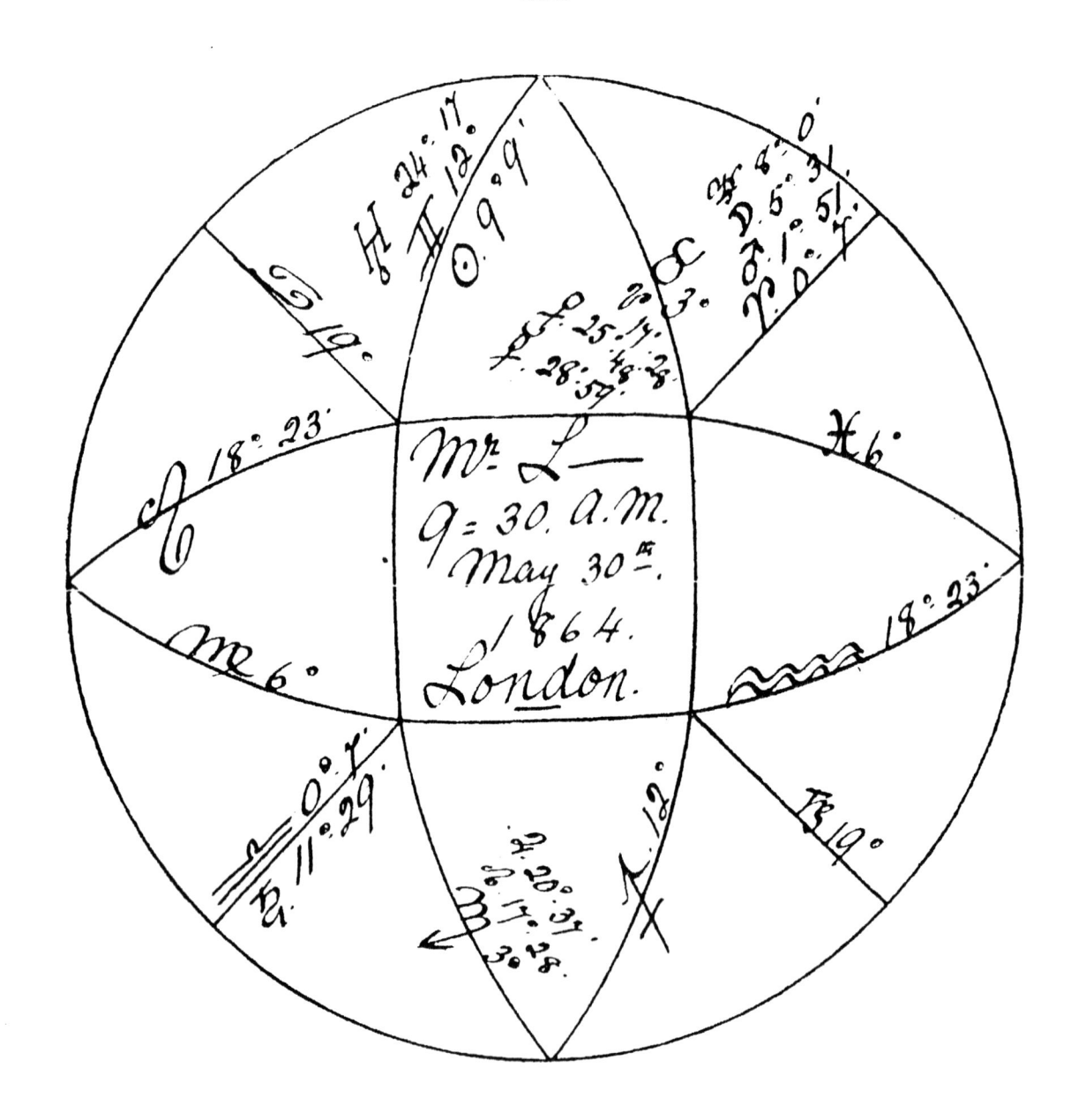

EXAMPLE: HOW TO CAST THE HOROSCOPE.

Mr. L—— was born at 9.30 a.m., May 30th, 1864, at London.

	H.	M.
Sidereal Time, May 30th	4	33
Subtract	2	30
	2	3

Seek in the Tables of Houses for the latitude of London 2h. 3m. and opposite will be found ♉ 3° M.C. (Meridian), ♊ 12° cusp of the 11th house and ♋ 19° cusp of the 12th house and ♌ 18° ascendant. ♍ 6° cusp of the 2nd house and ♎ 0°7' cusp of the 3rd house. The transposition of the planets from the Ephemeris to the horoscope is a very simple process. The Moon has travelled about 1 degree 27 minutes, the Sun 6 minutes, Venus 7 minutes in the 2½ hours which have elapsed since the birth and which should be deducted from their longitudes at noon.

Positions at Mr. L——'s 32nd birthday.

☉ 9°♋43'	☽ 9°♊17'	♆ 8°♈20'	♅ 26°♊11'	♄ 11°♎35'
♃ 18°♏0'	♂ 4°♈54'	♀ 5°♋0'	☿ 22°♊29'	☋ 15°♏6'

Positions at Mr. L——'s 34th birthday.

☉ 11°♋38'	☽ 4°♋31'	♆ 8°♈20'	♅ 26°♊18'	♄ 11°♎38'
♃ 17°♏55'	♂ 26°♈17'	♀ 7°♋27'	☿ 26°♊5'	☋ 15°♏39'

CHAPTER XXI.

HOW TO COMPUTE A HOROSCOPE FOR SOUTH LATITUDE.

N.B.—The adoption of Standard Time by New South Wales, Queensland, Tasmania and Victoria means that all through these zones a Standard Time is used calculated for a Meridian of 150 degrees of longitude east of Greenwich which is ten hours fast of Greenwich.

Therefore Brisbane is using a time which is twelve minutes later than its true local time and therefore on the birth of a child to-day this correction should be made, *viz.*: If a child is born at 12h. 30m. a.m., March 22nd, 1909, at Brisbane, then twelve minutes should be added thus:

```
    H.   M.
    12   30 a.m.
         12
    ─────────
    12   42
```

which would be the true local time at Brisbane.

Wanted the horoscope of a person born 12.30 a.m., March 22nd, 1866, Brisbane. Latitude 27° 30' south, longitude 153° 2' east.

R.A. noon, March 21st, 1866	23°	55'
Hours elapsed	12°	30'
	35°	85'
	36°	25'
For acceleration of sidereal time		2'
	36°	27'
Subtract the circle	24°	0
	12°	27'

126

If southern tables of houses are not available use northern ones for latitude 27°.

Seek 12° 27' and ♎ 8° will be found on the cusp of the 10th house. Then add twelve hours to the R.A. Thus:—

$$\begin{array}{rr} 12 & 27 \\ 12 & 0 \\ \hline 24 & 27 \\ 24 & 0 \\ \hline 0 & 27 \end{array}$$

Subtract the circle

Now seek 0° 27' in the tables of houses for north latitude 27°, and substitute ♎ 8° for ♈ 8°—♏ 12° for ♉ 12°— ♐ 17° for ♊ 17°—ascendant 18° ♑ for 18° ♋—11° ♒ for 11° ♌—7° ♓ for 7° ♍.

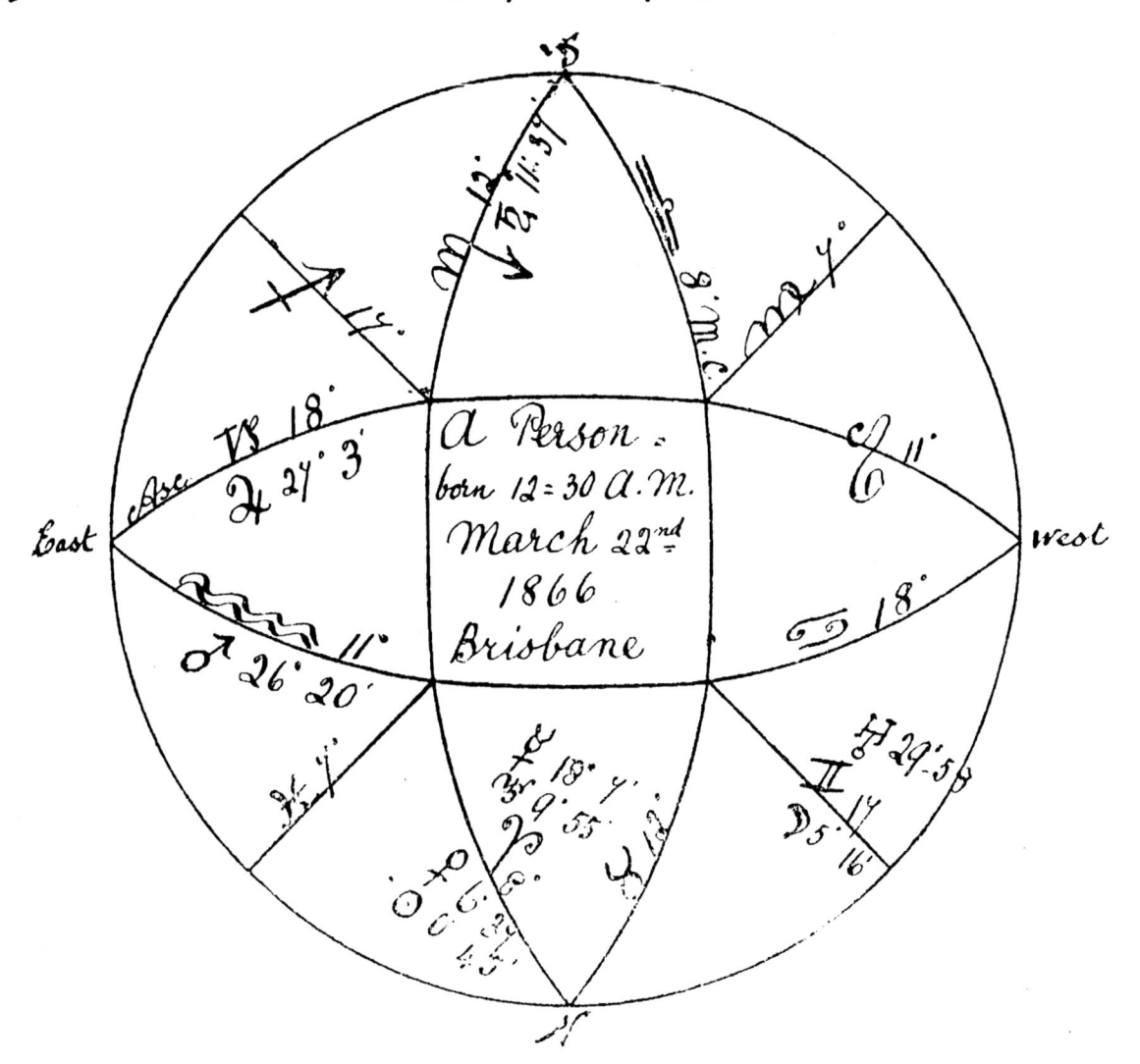

Half a degree equals 2 minutes and a quarter of a degree equals 1 minute, 1 degree equals 4 minutes of time, thus 15 degrees equal 1 hour. Thirty degrees equal two hours; 45 degrees equal 3 hours; 180 degrees equal 12 hours. Therefore 360 degrees equal 24 hours.

As far as we can ascertain since 1893 many countries adopted what is called Standard Time for Railway purposes and Navigation, thus Belgium, Great Britain, Holland, Portugal and Spain use since January, 1901, Greenwich time. Ireland the Meridian of Dublin, which is 25 minutes 22 seconds slow of Greenwich mean time.

France and Algeria meridian of Paris, which is 9 minutes 21 seconds fast of Greenwich.

Austria-Hungary, Denmark, Germany, Italy, Malta, Norway, Servia, Switzerland, Meridian of 15 E., or 1 hour fast of Greenwich, since April 1st, 1893.

Turkey uses Western European time for purposes of Navigation, which is Greenwich time, but her people still use the old method.

Russia 2 hours 1 minute E. of Greenwich.

Bulgaria and Roumania 2 hours E.

Egypt, Cape Colony, Natal, Transvaal, Orange River Colony, Rhodesia and Portuguese East Africa 2 hours E. of Greenwich. They advanced the time by 30 minutes in 1903.

Jersey adopted Greenwich time in June, 1898; Guernsey, April, 1909.

Mauritius and Seychelles.—On January 1st, 1907, Standard Time of 60th meridian, or 4 hours fast of Greenwich mean time adopted.

Chagos Islands.—On January 1st, 1907, Standard Time of 75th meridian, or 5 hours fast of Greenwich mean time adopted.

India and Ceylon.—Meridian of 82° 30' E., or 5½ hours fast of Greenwich mean time, since 1904.

Burmah.—Meridian of 97° 30' E., or 6½ hours fast of Greenwich mean time.

Straits Settlement and Malay Federated States.—Meridian of 105° E., or 7 hours fast of Greenwich mean time.

Hong Kong and East Coast of China.—Meridian of 120° E., or 8 hours fast of Greenwich mean time.

Japan.—Meridian of 135° E., or 9 hours fast of Greenwich mean time.

Shanghai, Kiau Chau, Philippine Islands, Western Australia.—Meridian of 120° E., or 8 hours fast of Greenwich mean time.

South Australia.—Meridian of 142° 30' E., or 9½ hours fast of Greenwich mean time.

New South Wales, Queensland, Tasmania, Victoria.—Meridian of 150° E., or 10 hours fast of Greenwich mean time.

New Zealand.—Meridian of 172½° E., or 11½ hours fast of Greenwich mean time.

Sandwich Islands.—Meridian of 157° 30' W., or 10½ hours slow of Greenwich mean time.

Ecuador.—Meridian of 81° 3′ 45″ W., or 5h. 24m. 15s. slow of Greenwich mean time.

Argentine Republic.—Meridian of Cordova, 4h. 16m. 48·2s. slow of Greenwich mean time.

New Brunswick, Nova Scotia, Prince Edward's Island, Porto Rico.—Meridian of 60° W., or 4 hours slow of Greenwich mean time.

Cuba.—Local mean time, and not standard time of the 75th meridian of W. long., is now in use in Cuba. The time ball in approximately 23° 8′ 27″ N., 82° 20′ 55″ W., at Havana, is dropped at local mean noon, corresponding to 5h. 29m. 23·7s. p.m. Greenwich mean time.

Canada and the United States.—In Canada and the United States, the territories are divided into hourly zones, the standard times for which are respectively 4, 5, 6, 7, and 8 hours slow of Greenwich, the corresponding meridians being 60°, 75°, 90°, 105° and 120° W. As a rule the time used in Canada, from the East coast to 67½° W., is 4 hours slow of Greenwich (Intercolonial time); between 67½° and 82½° W., 5 hours slow (Eastern time); between 82½° and 97½° W., 6 hours slow (Central time); between 97½° and 112½° W., 7 hours slow (Mountain time); from 112½° W. to the West coast, 8 hours slow of Greenwich (Pacific time).

British Columbia.—Meridian of 120° W., or 8 hours slow of Greenwich mean time.

The planets' places must be computed to equivalent Greenwich time.

Multiply the longitude of Brisbane by 4, and divide the sum by 60 thus:—

```
    153
      4
    ———
60)612(10
     60
    ———
     12
    ═══
```

We have 10h. 12m., which means that Brisbane's time is 10h. 12m. ahead of Greenwich.

Time.—When, therefore, it is 12.30 a.m. at Brisbane, it is 2.18 p.m. at Greenwich, March 21st, for which the planets' places should be computed.

For the last few years Australia has adopted a Standard Time; but we do not know the date of the adoption. The Standard Time differs from the true local time of Brisbane by 12 minutes. The Standard Time is computed for a Meridian of 150 degrees East Longitude of Greenwich; whereas the longitude of Brisbane is almost 153 degrees East. When, therefore, Standard Time is used in recording the birth time a correction of 12 minutes should be made, which means that 12 minutes should be added to the Standard Time.

We are unable to indicate the year when many countries adopted Standard Time.

Since the adoption of Standard Time a correction is necessary when using the Ephemeris computed for Greenwich time. Suppose a child was born at 1.10 p.m., September 29th, 1904, at Leipzig. As that town is using Middle European time 10 minutes should be deducted from the time used in recording the birth, because Leipzig's true local time is about 10 minutes later than Middle European time. The planets computed for noon Greenwich equals 1.10 p.m. Leipzig.

Greenwich time is used in most of the towns in England, Scotland and Wales, but the date of its adoption in the towns as well as at the railway stations is difficult to arrive at. Greenwich sent time current signals to a few stations on the South Eastern Railway in 1852 and in 1872 the Post Office sent the time signals to the provinces. Many provincial church clocks continued to keep true local time, hence they differed from station time. But somewhere between 1872 and 1880 there appears to have been a general adoption of Greenwich time by the churches.

EPHEMERIS FOR FEBRUARY, 1866.

D M	Neptune. Long.	Neptune. Declin.	Herschel. Lat.	Herschel. Declin.	Saturn. Lat.	Saturn. Declin.	Jupiter. Lat.	Jupiter. Declin.
	° ′	° ′	° ′	° ′	° ′	° ′	° ′	° ′
1	8♈21	1 N 55	0 N 16	23 N 43	2 N 26	13 S 9	0 S 5	22 S 22
4	8 25	1 57	0 16	23 43	2 26	13 9	0 5	22 17
7	8 30	1 59	0 16	23 43	2 27	13 10	0 5	22 12
10	8 35	2 1	0 16	23 43	2 27	13 10	0 6	22 7
13	8 40	2 3	0 16	23 43	2 28	13 11	0 6	22 1
16	8 46	2 5	0 16	23 43	2 29	13 10	0 6	21 56
19	8 51	2 7	0 16	23 43	2 30	13 10	0 7	21 51
22	8 57	2 10	0 16	23 43	2 31	13 9	0 7	21 45
25	9 2	2 12	0 16	23 43	2 32	13 8	0 7	21 40
28	9 8	2 14	0 16	23 43	2 33	13 7	0 8	21 34

D M	D W	Sidereal Time	☉ Long	☉ Declin.	☽ Long.	☽ Lat.	☽ Declin.	♅ Long.
		H. M. S.	° ′ ″	° ′	° ′	° ′	° ′	° ′
1	Th	20 45 52	12♒28 7	17 S 4	2♍21	3 S 21	7 N 31	0♋24
2	F	20 49 48	13 28 57	16 47	15 1	2 26	3 40	0℞23
3	S	20 53 45	14 29 46	16 30	27 23	1 25	0 S 15	0 22
4	𝕾	20 57 41	15 30 34	16 12	9♎31	0 21	4 5	0 20
5	M	21 1 38	16 31 20	15 54	21 28	0 N 43	7 42	0 19
6	Tu	21 5 34	17 32 6	15 35	3♏17	1 45	10 58	0 18
7	W	21 9 31	18 32 51	15 17	15 6	2 42	13 47	0 16
8	Th	21 13 27	19 33 34	14 58	26 58	3 33	16 3	0 15
9	F	21 17 24	20 34 17	14 39	8♐59	4 14	17 37	0 13
10	S	21 21 21	21 34 59	14 19	21 15	4 45	18 25	0 12
11	𝕾	21 25 17	22 35 39	13 59	3♑49	5 3	18 21	0 11
12	M	21 29 14	23 36 18	13 40	16 44	5 7	17 20	0 10
13	Tu	21 33 10	24 36 56	13 19	0♒1	4 54	15 22	0 8
14	W	21 37 7	25 37 33	12 59	13 39	4 24	12 31	0 7
15	Th	21 41 3	26 38 8	12 39	27 37	3 39	8 53	0 6
16	F	21 45 0	27 38 41	12 18	11♓48	2 38	4 42	0 4
17	S	21 48 56	28 39 13	11 57	26 10	1 27	0 11	0 3
18	𝕾	21 52 53	29 39 43	11 36	10♈35	0 10	4 N 21	0 2
19	M	21 56 49	0♓40 11	11 15	24 59	1 S 7	8 38	0 1
20	Tu	22 0 46	1 40 38	10 53	9♉19	2 21	12 23	0 1
21	W	22 4 43	2 41 2	10 31	23 32	3 25	15 22	0 0
22	Th	22 8 39	3 41 25	10 10	7♊36	4 15	17 23	29♊59
23	F	22 12 36	4 41 46	9 48	21 30	4 51	18 21	29 59
24	S	22 16 32	5 42 4	9 26	5♋13	5 9	18 12	29 58
25	𝕾	22 20 29	6 42 21	9 3	18 45	5 9	17 2	29 57
26	M	22 24 25	7 42 35	8 41	2♌5	4 53	14 57	29 57
27	Tu	22 28 22	8 42 48	8 18	15 13	4 22	12 7	29 56
28	W	22 32 18	9 42 58	7 56	28 7	3 37	8 44	29 56

EPHEMERIS FOR FEBRUARY, 1866.

D M	Mars. Lat.	Mars. Declin.	Venus. Lat.	Venus. Declin.	Mercury. Lat.	Mercury. Declin.
	° ′	° ′	° ′	° ′	° ′	° ′
1	0 S 49	22 S 53	0 S 59	19 S 37	1 S 5	22 S 24
4	0 51	22 34	1 4	18 43	1 22	21 50
7	0 53	22 13	1 9	17 44	1 37	21 4
10	0 55	21 49	1 13	16 40	1 48	20 6
13	0 56	21 24	1 16	15 32	1 58	18 56
16	0 58	20 56	1 19	14 20	2 3	17 33
19	0 59	20 26	1 21	13 5	2 6	15 57
22	1 1	19 55	1 23	11 47	2 4	14 9
25	1 2	19 21	1 25	10 26	2 0	12 8
28	1 4	18 46	1 26	9 2	1 49	9 55

D M	♄ Long.	♃ Long.	♂ Long.	♀ Long.	☿ Long.	Mutual Aspects.	Lunar Aspects. ☉	♅	♄	♃	♂	♀	☿
	° ′	° ′	° ′	° ′	° ′								
1	12 ♏ 2	17 ♑ 40	19 ♑ 16	6 ♒ 30	23 ♑ 54	☉ □ ♄		✱					
2	12 4	17 53	20 2	7 45	25 23				✱	△	△		
3	12 6	18 6	20 48	9 0	26 53			□					△
4	12 8	18 19	21 33	10 15	28 24	☉ ⚼ ♅						△	
5	12 9	18 33	22 19	11 31	29 55	♀ □ ♄	△			□	□		
6	12 11	18 46	23 5	12 46	1 ♒ 27			△					□
7	12 12	18 59	23 51	14 1	3 0	♂ P. ♃	□		☌	✱		□	
8	12 13	19 12	24 37	15 16	4 34	♀ ⚼ ♅					✱		
9	12 14	19 25	25 23	16 32	6 9								✱
10	12 15	19 38	26 9	17 47	7 44		✱					✱	
11	12 16	19 51	26 55	19 2	9 20			☍					
12	12 17	20 2	27 41	20 17	10 57				✱	☌			
13	12 18	20 16	28 27	21 33	12 36	☿ □ ♄					☌		
14	12 19	20 29	29 13	22 48	14 15				□				☌
15	12 19	20 41	29 59	24 3	15 54	☿ ⚼ ♅	☌	△				☌	
16	12 20	20 53	0 ♒ 45	25 18	17 35				△				
17	12 20	21 6	1 31	26 33	19 17			□		✱	✱		
18	12 20	21 18	2 17	27 48	20 59	☉ △ ♅							
19	12 21	21 30	3 4	29 4	22 42	♄ P. ♀	✱	✱		□		✱	✱
20	12 21	21 43	3 50	0 ♓ 19	24 27	♀ △ ♅			☍		□		
21	12 ℞ 21	21 55	4 36	1 34	26 12					△			□
22	12 20	22 7	5 22	2 49	27 58		□				△	□	
23	12 20	22 19	6 8	4 4	29 46	☿ △ ♅							
24	12 19	22 31	6 54	5 19	1 ♓ 34		△	☌				△	△
25	12 19	22 43	7 41	6 34	3 23	☉ ☌ ♀			△	☍			
26	12 18	22 55	8 27	7 49	5 13						☍		
27	12 17	23 7	9 14	9 4	7 4				□				
28	12 16	23 19	10 0	10 19	8 56	☿ ∠ ♃		✱					

EPHEMERIS FOR MARCH, 1866.

D M	Neptune. Long.	Neptune. Declin.	Herschel. Lat.	Herschel. Declin.	Saturn. Lat.	Saturn. Declin.	Jupiter. Lat.	Jupiter. Declin.
	° ′	° ′	° ′	° ′	° ′	° ′	° ′	° ′
1	9♈10	2N15	0N16	23N43	2N33	13S 6	0S 8	21S32
4	9 16	2 17	0 16	23 43	2 33	13 5	0 8	21 27
7	9 22	2 20	0 16	23 43	2 34	13 3	0 8	21 21
10	9 29	2 23	0 16	23 43	2 34	13 0	0 9	21 16
13	9 35	2 25	0 16	23 43	2 35	12 58	0 9	21 10
16	9 42	2 28	0 16	23 43	2 35	12 55	0 10	21 5
19	9 50	2 31	0 16	23 43	2 36	12 53	0 10	20 59
22	9 57	2 34	0 16	23 43	2 36	12 50	0 11	20 54
25	10 4	2 36	0 16	23 43	2 37	12 46	0 11	20 49
28	10 10	2 39	0 16	23 43	2 37	12 43	0 12	20 44
31	10 17	2 42	0 16	23 43	2 38	12 39	0 12	20 39

D M	D W	Sidereal Time.	☉ Long.	☉ Declin.	☽ Long.	☽ Lat.	☽ Declin.	♅ Long.
		H. M. S.	° ′ ″	° ′	° ′	° ′	° ′	° ′
1	Th	22 36 15	10♓43 8	7S33	10♍47	2S43	5N 1	29♊55
2	F	22 40 12	11 43 14	7 10	23 13	1 41	1 9	29℞55
3	S	22 44 8	12 43 20	6 47	5♎27	0 36	2S43	29 54
4	𝕾	22 48 5	13 43 23	6 24	17 30	0N30	6 24	29 54
5	M	22 52 1	14 43 25	6 1	29 24	1 35	9 48	29 54
6	Tu	22 55 58	15 43 25	5 38	11♏14	2 34	12 46	29 53
7	W	22 59 54	16 43 23	5 15	23 2	3 27	15 12	29 53
8	Th	23 3 51	17 43 20	4 51	4♐55	4 12	17 0	29D23
9	F	23 7 47	18 43 15	4 28	16 55	4 46	18 4	29 53
10	S	23 11 44	19 43 8	4 4	29 9	5 8	18 19	29 53
11	𝕾	23 15 41	20 43 0	3 41	11♑41	5 16	17 42	29 53
12	M	23 19 37	21 42 50	3 17	24 35	5 8	16 10	29 54
13	Tu	23 23 34	22 42 38	2 54	7♒53	4 44	13 44	29 54
14	W	23 27 30	23 42 25	2 30	21 37	4 3	10 28	29 55
15	Th	23 31 27	24 42 9	2 6	5♓45	3 7	6 31	29 55
16	F	23 35 23	25 41 52	1 43	20 13	1 57	2 5	29 56
17	S	23 39 20	26 41 33	1 19	4♈57	0 38	2N33	29 56
18	𝕾	23 43 16	27 41 12	0 55	19 48	0S44	7 4	29 57
19	M	23 47 13	28 40 48	0 32	4♉39	2 3	11 9	29 57
20	Tu	23 51 10	29 40 22	0 8	19 23	3 14	14 29	29 58
21	W	23 55 6	0♈39 55	0N16	3♊54	4 10	16 50	29 58
22	Th	23 59 3	1 39 24	0 40	18 9	4 51	18 6	29 59
23	F	0 2 59	2 38 52	1 3	2♋ 6	5 13	18 13	0♋ 0
24	S	0 6 56	3 38 17	1 27	15 43	5 17	17 17	0 1
25	𝕾	0 10 52	4 37 40	1 50	29 2	5 3	15 25	0 2
26	M	0 14 49	5 37 0	2 14	12♌ 4	4 35	12 47	0 3
27	Tu	0 18 45	6 36 18	2 37	24 51	3 53	9 35	0 4
28	W	0 22 42	7 35 34	3 1	7♍24	3 0	6 1	0 5
29	Th	0 26 38	8 34 48	3 24	19 45	2 0	2 13	0 6
30	F	0 30 35	9 33 59	3 48	1♎56	0 55	1 S37	0 7
31	S	0 34 32	10 33 9	4 11	13 59	0N12	5 20	0 8

EPHEMERIS FOR MARCH, 1866.

D M	Mars Lat.	Mars Declin.	Venus Lat.	Venus Declin.	Mercury Lat.	Mercury Declin.
	° ′	° ′	° ′	° ′	° ′	° ′
1	1 S 4	18 S 33	1 S 26	8 S 33	1 S 45	9 S 8
4	1 5	17 56	1 26	7 7	1 27	6 40
7	1 6	17 16	1 26	5 39	1 7	4 3
10	1 7	16 35	1 25	4 9	0 44	1 18
13	1 8	15 53	1 23	2 39	0 14	1 N 30
16	1 9	15 9	1 21	1 7	0 N 23	4 15
19	1 10	14 23	1 18	0 N 24	1 4	6 51
22	1 11	13 37	1 15	1 56	1 44	9 11
25	1 12	12 49	1 11	3 27	2 16	11 9
28	1 13	12 0	1 7	4 58	2 42	12 38
31	1 14	11 10	1 2	6 28	3 3	13 37

D M	♄ Long.	♃ Long.	♂ Long.	♀ Long.	☿ Long.	Mutual Aspects.	Lunar Aspects. ☉	♅	♄	♃	♂	♀	☿
	° ′	° ′	° ′	° ′	° ′								
1	12 ♏ 15	23 ♑ 30	10 ♒ 47	11 ♓ 34	10 ♓ 50	☉ ☌ ☿	☍		✱			☍	☍
2	12 ℞ 14	23 41	11 33	12 49	12 44	☿ △ ♄				△			
3	12 13	23 52	12 20	14 4	14 38	♂ □ ♄		□					
4	12 12	24 4	13 6	15 19	16 34						△		
5	12 10	24 15	13 53	16 33	18 30			△		□			
6	12 9	24 26	14 39	17 48	20 27	♂ ⚼ ♅	△		☌		□		
7	12 7	24 38	15 26	19 3	22 24					✱		△	△
8	12 6	24 49	16 12	20 18	24 21	♀ ✱ ♃							
9	12 4	25 0	16 59	21 33	26 19	☿ ⚼ ♄	□				✱	□	
10	12 2	25 11	17 45	22 48	28 17			☍					□
11	12 0	25 22	18 32	24 3	0 ♈ 13	☿ □ ♅			✱				
12	11 58	25 33	19 18	25 18	2 9	♀ ✱ ♃	✱			☌		✱	
13	11 56	25 43	20 5	26 32	4 4	♀ ⚼ ♄			□				✱
14	11 54	25 54	20 51	27 47	5 58	☿ ∠ ♂					☌		
15	11 52	26 4	21 38	29 1	7 50			△	△				
16	11 50	26 14	22 24	0 ♈ 16	9 40	♀ □ ♅	☌			✱			
17	11 47	26 24	23 11	1 31	11 27	☉ ✱ ♃		□				☌	☌
18	11 45	26 34	23 57	2 46	13 11					□	✱		
19	11 42	26 44	24 44	4 0	14 51	☉ P. ♀		✱					
20	11 39	26 54	25 30	5 15	16 28	☉ □ ♅			☍		□		
21	11 37	27 3	26 17	6 30	18 0		✱			△		✱	
22	11 34	27 12	27 4	7 44	19 27								✱
23	11 31	27 22	27 51	8 59	20 48		□	☌			△		
24	11 28	27 31	28 37	10 14	22 4				△			□	
25	11 25	27 40	29 24	11 28	23 14	♂ P. ♄	△			☍			□
26	11 22	27 49	0 ♓ 10	12 43	24 18	♂ △ ♅			□			△	
27	11 19	27 58	0 57	13 57	25 15			✱			☍		△
28	11 15	28 7	1 43	15 12	26 5				✱				
29	11 12	28 16	2 30	16 26	26 49								
30	11 9	28 24	3 16	17 40	27 25			□		△			
31	11 5	28 33	4 3	18 55	27 54	♀ ∠ ♂	☍					☍	

From Mr. W. T. Stead's "Review of Reviews."

"In the year 1884 a dark-haired, short-sighted lad of 18 might have been seen cycling rapidly thirty miles from Drayton, near Bletchley, to Bedford. He carried in his pocket the newly issued number of *Tit-Bits*, one column of which he had eagerly scanned before he had mounted his cycle, and the contents of which were revolving in his busy brain as rapidly as the wheels of his cycle along the roads. The moment he arrived at Bedford he made for the County Library, and for the rest of the day remained immersed in dictionaries, cyclopædias, gazetteers and all the other storehouses of condensed literary pemmican which were to be found on its shelves. It was difficult for the casual visitor to divine the reason for his omnivorous quest for information. He was not pursuing any particular line of study, for his investigation ranged over the most diverse fields of human knowledge.

"All that he wanted was to obtain the answer to each of these one hundred and thirty questions, propounded at the rate of ten every week, and arbitrarily fixed by the sphinx of *Tit-Bits*. As soon as he had worked his way by the aid of much industrious research through the list of questions he remounted his cycle and pedalled back across the country to his father's rectory. Once a week for three months he made this pilgrimage and duly, after each visit to the Bedford County Library, he posted to Mr. Newnes's editor (in an envelope marked 'Inquiry Column') a list of answers accurately filled in according to the best of his knowledge and belief. This assiduous industry and punctuality were induced by an offer made by Mr. Newnes to the world in general to give the person who most accurately answered the questions published in thirteen consecutive weeks of his journal a situation in his office with a salary to start with of £100 a year. The situation was guaranteed for one year, but could be obtained only on condition of references as to honesty being furnished. The competition opened on May 31st and ended August 23rd, and when it closed there ensued a period of painful suspense.

"Three thousand competitors from all parts of the kingdom had been engaged in filling in answers to their papers week by week, so that the editor in London had no fewer than 39,000 examination papers to go through before he could adjudicate the winner in the competition.

"At last on the eventful day (only delayed a fortnight) the award was published, when it was discovered that Mr. Cyril Arthur Pearson, of Drayton Parslow Rectory, Bletchley Station, had come out top, with 414 marks to his credit. The next competitor (Mr. F. S. Knowles) had secured 362 marks. Mr. Cyril Arthur Pearson was none other than the dark-haired, short-sighted youth who in the course of three months had cycled

780 miles in order to visit the nearest library from which he could obtain the information which was to give him his first step in the ladder of life. At the age of 18, in September, 1884, Mr. Pearson was installed accordingly as clerk in the office of Mr. (now Sir George) Newnes, the editor and proprietor of *Tit-Bits*. He rapidly won his way into the good graces of his employer. He was industrious, punctual, a demon of energy, who made up his mind that having obtained his chance he would make the most of it. Mr. Newnes appreciated his capacity, but even he was hardly prepared for the ambition of the youth whom he was introducing to the wider world. Hence it was with profound surprise that he received Mr. Pearson's application for the managership of *Tit-Bits* when, six months after his arrival in the office, a vacancy occurred in that post. *Tit-Bits* was not then what it is now, but it was even then (in its fifth year) a great and flourishing concern. Mr. Newnes was at first considerably staggered by the impudence of the youth who, at the age of 19, aspired to manage *Tit-Bits*, but Mr. Pearson in his frank, brisk way, with his persuasive argument, succeeded in inducing his employer to give him an opportunity of showing what he could do. Hence it was that at the age of 19 Mr. Pearson was manager of *Tit-Bits*. Mr. Pearson continued to run *Tit-Bits* for Mr. Newnes until the end of 1889 at a salary of £300 a year. Mr. Pearson applied to Sir George Newnes for an increase of salary. Sir George refused, whereupon Mr. Pearson shook the dust off his feet and departed to found *Pearson's Weekly*.

"He took offices in Temple Chambers, Temple Avenue, engaged a cashier, borrowed £3,000 from a friend and founded *Pearson's Weekly*. It was larger than *Tit-Bits*, with more liberal inducements to subscribers in the shape of insurances and prizes, but was in all essentials built upon *Tit-Bits* lines. The paper was successful from the start, and everything was booming, when suddenly the financial bottom fell out of the concern. His friend who had financed the paper at the beginning had got hit in the Argentine speculations and wanted his money back. Mr. Pearson, however, was not a man to be daunted by this difficulty. He rushed round seeking for the necessary capital and by good fortune was led to seek the help of Sir William Ingram of the *Illustrated London News*. Sir William supplied the money, with which Mr. Pearson paid off the original loan, and he and Mr. Keary (who was then taken into the firm) devoted themselves to building up the success of *Pearson's Weekly*.

"In July, 1898, Pearson's business was converted into a limited liability company, with a share capital of £400,000. The ordinary stock of 125,000 £1 shares was held entirely by the original members of the firm, Mr. Pearson, Sir William Ingram, and Mr. Keary. Fifty thousand 5½ per cent. preference shares of £5 each were eagerly subscribed by the public, nor have those who selected Pearson's as a mode of investment had any reason to regret their confidence in his business. The following table shows the amount of profit declared each financial year ending 31st May: 1897, £40,874; 1898, £42,649; 1899, £44,998."

"A very creditable first number was the *Daily Express*, which owes its origin to the enterprise, energy and journalistic ambition of Mr. Pearson. According to the statements published in the second number, the orders for No. 1 surpassed all records, no fewer than a million and a half copies having been demanded as a means of satisfying the public curiosity. To turn out so huge a mass of printed matter as the eight hundred thousand odd which were actually produced before the machines gave out on the very first day of going to press was an achievement upon which Mr. Pearson naturally prided himself. That he will be able to keep up the circulation to anything approaching that figure is not to be hoped for. No paper prints a million and a half a day in any part of the world. To print eight hundred thousand on the first day on which the paper was offered to the public was a record in the journalism of the world."

"Yes," said Mr. Pearson, "I am Editor as well as proprietor. Surely the recent experience of the *Daily Chronicle* is sufficient to convince anyone that the combination of offices is the only security for continuity of purpose and of policy in the editing of a paper. I do not mean to say," continued Mr. Pearson cheerfully, "that I am sole proprietor. I hold about 75 per cent. of the stock. The rest is shared by two persons—my partner, Mr. Keary, of Henrietta Street, and one other, whose holding, however, is not sufficient to enable him to influence the policy of the paper, even if he so desired it. Practically I am my own proprietor, a position which every editor covets and which very few are fortunate enough to attain."

INSTRUCTIONS IN THE CALCULATIONS OF STAR COURSES.

CHAPTER XXII.

Lesson I.

THE time measure we use is the Chaldean time measure in which a day is counted as a year of life, that is to say, the motions of the Planets, of the Sun and Moon in the first 24 hours after a child's birth represent that child's first year of life. Therefore, its fifth day represents its fifth year. The motions of the Planets on the tenth day represent the child's tenth year.

It will be observed that the subject of the test horoscope (who turned out to be Mr. C. Arthur Pearson) won his clerkship at the age of 18 years and 7 months, for he was installed in the office of Sir George Newnes in September, 1884. We will, therefore, calculate the Star Courses to the nineteenth year.

We begin by counting 19 days from the day of birth. Mr. Pearson was born on February 24th, 1866, therefore March 15th will be his nineteenth year. Therefore, we calculate the Planets' Places for 11 a.m. on March 15th, 1866, and we have the Planets' Places corresponding to the nineteenth year of Mr. Pearson's life.

We place the signs on the cusps of the Houses as they are in the original horoscope. The Planets' Places we calculate as follows: The Sun's motion in 24 hours is 1°, which is very nearly 2 minutes in one hour. We, therefore, subtract 2 minutes from the Sun's longitude and we have the Sun's longitude at 11 a.m. 24°40'.

The Moon's motion in 24 hours is 14°8' which is easily ascertained by subtracting the longitude of the Moon on March 14th from the longitude of the Moon on March 15th. Then the proportional logarithm of 14°8' is - .2300   and the proportional logarithm of one hour is - - 1.3802   Then by adding these together

we have - - 1.6102

The nearest proportional logarithm to 1.6102 is 1.6143, and opposite to this number is 35 minutes, and these must be deducted from the Moon's longitude at noon, March 15th, 1866. Thus:

   Moon - - 5°45' Pisces.
   Less - -   35'
            ———
   Moon - - 5°10' Pisces.

Neptune, Uranus, Saturn and Jupiter move so slowly that there is nothing to deduct from their longitudes.

The motion of Mars is 47' in 24 hours, which is almost exactly 2 minutes in one hour. Therefore, we deduct 2 minutes from the longitude of Mars at noon, March 15th, 1866, which makes the longitude at 11 a.m. 21°26'.

Wanted the longitude of Venus at 11 a.m., March 15th, 1866. The longitude of Venus on March 14th was - 27°47' Pisces.
On March 15th it was - - - - 29° 1' Pisces.

By subtracting one from the other we have the motion of Venus in 24 hours 1°14'.

The proportional logarithm of 1°14' = 1.2891, and the proportional logarithm of one hour is - - 1.3802

which added together - - = 2.6693

The nearest proportional logarithm to this is 2.6812, and opposite this we have 3 minutes which means that 3 minutes must be deducted from the longitude of Venus at noon, for as she moves 3 minutes in one hour if we deduct 3 minutes from her longitude at noon we have her longitude at 11 a.m., March 15th, 1866, which equals 28°58' Pisces.

Wanted the longitude of Mercury at 11 a.m., March 15th, 1866.
Longitude of Mercury, March 15th - - 7°50' Aries.
 ,, ,,   March 14th - - 5°58' ,,
By deducting one from the other the motion of ———
Mercury in 24 hours - - - 1°52'

That is to say, Mercury has moved 1°52' in 24 hours. What we want to know is how far will Mercury move in one hour.

  The proportional logarithm of 1°52' = 1.1091
  The proportional logarithm of one hour = 1.3802
              ———
We add these together and we have - 2.4893

The nearest proportional logarithm number to this is 2.4594 and opposite to this we have 5 minutes which means that Mercury has travelled 5 minutes in one hour and we subtract 5 minutes from Mercury's longitude at noon on March 15th. Thus Mercury's longitude on March 15th is 7°50' Aries, 5 minutes from this leaves 7°45' Aries.

Rule.—Find the daily motion of the planet. Add the proportional log. of this motion to the log. of the time from noon and the total will be the log. of the required motion. If the time be p.m. add this motion to the planet's place at noon, but subtract if a.m., and the total or remainder will be the planet's place at the required time. If the planet should be retrograde (which can be seen from the Ephemeris) subtract for p.m. and add for a.m.

Example : Wanted Moon's longitude June 1st, 1893, at 10.20 p.m.

Moon's long. noon. June 2nd - - 13°28' Capricorn
,,   ,,   ,,   1st - - 1°28'

Motion in 24 hours - - - - 12°
The proportional logarithm of 12° is - 30.10
,,   ,,   ,,   10h. 20m. is 36.60

66.70 which = 5°10'

The Moon's motion in 10h. 20m. is thus 5°10' which must be added to the Moon's longitude at noon, June 1st, 1893

Moon's long. June 1st   1°28' Capricorn
                         5°10'

Moon's long. 10.20 p.m. 6°38' Capricorn

As Tables of Houses and Logarithms are found at the end of Raphael's Ephemerides it is not necessary to reproduce them here. The price of an Ephemeris is 1/-.

Mr. Pearson started *Pearson's Weekly* at age 24. We will, therefore, reckon the 24th day after birth as the 24th year of life. This brings us to March 20th, 1866.

The longitude of the Sun at noon on March 20th is 29°40'. We therefore, deduct 2 minutes from that, for 2 minutes is the distance travelled by the Sun in one hour very nearly.

The Moon on March 19th is 4°39' Taurus, on the 20th the Moon is 19°23' Taurus. By subtracting the longitude on the 19th from the longitude on the 20th the Moon's motion is found to be 14°44'. The proportional logarithm

of 14°44' is - - - .2119
The proportional log. of 1 h. 1.3802   By adding these together

the sum is - - - 1·5921

The nearest proportional logarithm to this number is 1·5902 which is opposite to 37 minutes, which means that the Moon has travelled in one hour 37 minutes, which must be deducted from the Moon's longitude at noon, March 20th, 1866. Thus:

Moon   19° 23' Taurus
less   37'

18° 46' Taurus

which is the Moon's longitude at 11 a.m. March 20th, 1866.

Neptune, Uranus, Saturn and Jupiter move so slowly that there is nothing to deduct for one hour, consequently their longitude is put down exactly as it is found in the Ephemeris at noon.

The distance travelled by Mars in 24 hours is only 46', which is approximately 2 minutes for each hour, consequently we deduct 2 minutes from the longitude of Mars at noon, which makes it 25° 28'.

The longitude of Venus on March 20th is   5° 15' Aries
,,   ,,   ,,   ,, 19th ,, 4° 0' ,,

By subtracting one from the other the distance travelled by Venus in 24 hours is 1° 15'. The

Proportional logarithm for 1° 15' is -   -   1.2833
The proportional logarithm for 1 hour is -   1.3802

Which added together makes -   -   2.6635

The nearest number to this is 2.6812 and opposite this number is 3 minutes, which means that Venus has travelled 3 minutes in one hour. We, therefore, deduct 3 minutes from the longitude of Venus at noon, which makes the longitude of Venus at 11 a.m. 5° 12' Aries.

The longitude of Mercury at noon on March 20th is 16° 28' Aries, the longitude of Mercury at noon on March 19th is 14° 51' Aries. By subtracting 14° 51' from 16° 28' we have 1° 37', which means that the distance travelled by Mercury in 24 hours is 1° 37'. The proportional logarithm of 1° 37'

is -   1.1716   The proportional logarithm of one hour
is -   1.3802   By adding these together we

have 2.5518

The nearest proportional logarithm to this number is 2.5563 and opposite to this number is 4 minutes, which means that Mercury has travelled 4 minutes in one hour. We, therefore, deduct 4 minutes from the longitude of Mercury on March 26th, 1866, which makes the longitude of Mercury at 11 a.m. 16° 24' Aries.

It will be observed that Mr. Pearson started his paper the *Daily Express* at age 34. We, therefore, take the 34th day after birth, which brings us to March 30th, the Star Courses at that period representing the 34th year.

N.B.—Those who do not care to use logarithms can use the rule of three.

We deduct from the Sun's place 2 minutes, which is its motion in one hour. If the Moon moves 12° 11' in 24 hours she will move 12° 11' divided by 24 hours in one hour, which equals 30' 27". This deducted from 1° 56' on March 30th, 1866, equals 1° 26' Libra, which is the Moon's position on Mr. Pearson's 34th year.

Neptune, Uranus, Saturn and Jupiter have not moved a minute in the hour, consequently we take them direct from the Ephemeris.

As Mars has travelled 46 minutes we must again deduct 2 minutes from his longitude at noon on March 30th, 1866, which makes his longitude to be 3° 14' Pisces.

Venus on the 29th is 16° 26' Aries, on the 30th 17° 40' Aries. The distance travelled by Venus, therefore, in 24 hours is 1° 14'. As Venus travels 1° 14' in 24 hours she will travel 1° 14' divided by 24 in one hour, which equals 3'. This deducted from 17° 40' on March 30th, 1866, equals 7° 37' Aries, Venus' position on Mr. Pearson's 34th birthday.

If Mercury travels 0° 36' in 24 hours he will travel 0° 36' divided by 24 in one hour, which equals 1'. Therefore, by subtracting 1' from 27° 25' the longitude of Mercury at noon on March 30th, 1866, we have 27° 24' Aries, this being Mercury's position on March 30th, 1866.

Star Courses: Examples and Lessons.

We give an example of the Star Courses for the third year, when Mr. Pearson admits that he suffered in health. It will be observed that the Moon met the opposition of Mars and the square of Saturn. This is an instance where these aspects (which are Non-Promittors) caused some indisposition to a child of tender years; the same aspects have not exerted that power in later years when Mr. Pearson grew stronger: but at ages 13 and 14, when Mars by transit came to the opposition of Saturn and was retrograde, he had an attack of scarlet fever, and at age 18, when Mars by transit reached the quartile aspect of Saturn and was again retrograde, Mr. Pearson was badly hit on the head playing hockey. Of course Mars and Saturn are in square aspect at birth and are evil Promittors, *i.e.*, they promise accidents, bodily hurts, consequently every adverse transit of Mars to the place of Saturn in the horoscope threatens hurts and falls, and the adverse influence of Saturn and Mars was aggravated in the eighteenth year by the Moon's cross aspect to Saturn and its conjunction with Mars and the semi-square of the Sun to Mars' place in the radix. It will be observed that Mercury was in good aspect to Venus and the Sun, namely, the semi-sextile. These Promittors laid the foundation of his fortune, aided by the constantly recurring Promittors' good aspects to the Moon. It will be observed that before these good aspects of Mercury and Venus to the Sun had ceased to be operative he applied for and obtained the managership of *Tit-Bits* at a salary of £300 a year.

In the 23rd and 24th years, when Mr. Pearson founded *Pearson's Weekly*, Venus had reached the semi-sextile of the Sun in the horoscope, the Moon was entering the sign Taurus and forming a sextile to Mercury, Venus and the Sun in the horoscope, and in the 24th year he had still Venus in semi-sextile to the Sun in the radix, consequently he continued to increase the circulation of his publication. It will be noticed that the Sun was in quartile aspect to Uranus and in sesqui-quadrate to Saturn; but as these were not evil Promittors at birth they proved impotent. The Sun was in semi-quintile to Mars and the Sun was also in septile aspect to Mars, this aspect of a powerful Promittor is the aspect of much physical activity and energy, it is a most desirable aspect for projects requiring energy and executive power. The Sun in semi-sextile to Mars at birth (the Sun being on the Meridian) has great power, it is invariably the aspect of courage, and one needs no small amount of courage to found a periodical when part of the capital has to be borrowed.

He founded *Home Notes* at age 28, when the Sun was in semi-sextile to Mercury, and Venus was in semi-sextile to the Sun, the Sun was also in semi-quintile to Mars.

At age 30, when he founded his *Pearson's Magazine*, the Sun was in exact semi-sextile to Venus, and Venus was semi-quintile Sun, in sextile to Mars and in biquintile to Saturn; it will be noted that in the early months the Moon was in biquintile to the Sun in the radix and in trine to the Sun's progressive place in the middle months—truly most propitious aspects for the ventures. It will be admitted, therefore, that minor aspects of Promittors to the Sun have great power, they invariably confer much prosperity. Mr. Pearson's efforts invariably coincided with aspects of Promittors, which is remarkable since he consulted no astrologer.

When Mr. Pearson founded the *Daily Express* in his 34th year Mercury had reached the septile of the Sun in the horoscope, the Sun was in semi-quintile to Mars and the Sun was applying to the semi-quintile of Venus in the horoscope. Here again Mr. Pearson's venture coincided with the good aspects of Promittors. It will be remarked that the Sun was conjoined with Neptune and that Mars was very near to the Sun's place in the horoscope; but these aspects of Non-Promittors had not even the power to retard his progress, for they did not appear to be in the slightest degree operative.

Mr. Pearson's life since his 19th year has been a strenuous one, and some years ago Mr. Stead wrote to us telling us that Mr. Pearson was suffering from weakness of sight brought about by straining the eyes too much by reading in artificial light. Mr. Stead thought it would comfort Mr. Pearson to know if there was no danger of losing his eyesight. We assured Mr. Stead that there was not the slightest indication of blindness in the horoscope and that his eye trouble was the result of debility and overwork. We assured him that Mr. Pearson would be all right again very shortly; this pleasing intelligence was conveyed by Mr. Stead to Mr. Pearson and our prognostication was verified, for his eye trouble disappeared. Mr. Pearson should not attempt extensive reading by artificial light, for there is always the probability that he has inherited eyesight failings or weakness of sight, and if this is the case whenever he is run down or there is debility he will have trouble with his eyes. It is a fact that whenever there is debility the effects are felt in those parts of the body which are afflicted horoscopically or which have inherited some defect or weakness. The student will note that when we were wrong in our predictions we had attributed too much power to the adverse aspects of Non-Promittors.

Transits.

A planet exerts little power unless it is stationary, retrograde, or moving very slowly.

A Transit is the passage of a planet over some important or vital point in the horoscope or the progressive position of the Sun in the Star Courses. Such points of consequence are the places of the Sun, Moon, Ascendant and Mid-heaven and the Sun's progressive place. The other places of import are the places of Promittors themselves, which become active when incited by their own transiting force. It must not be forgotten that a beneficial transit of Jupiter would do much to modify a bad transit of Saturn with which it coincided. No change should be made or journey undertaken or new venture started coinciding with an adverse transit of such an adverse Promittor as Saturn.

The transits of Non-Promittors are rarely productive; therefore, unless a planet is in aspect to the Sun or Moon, or is in the Mid-heaven or Ascendant, it will not be likely to prove operative in its subsequent transits. Saturn has, however, in his transit over the Sun (when he has been retrograde) caused slight indisposition; but even this, the most powerful malefic, rarely causes trouble unless he afflicts one or both the luminaries in the horoscope. When Saturn is found to be stationary on the Sun's place he exerts much power for evil.

Transits of Promittors.

The transit of Jupiter over the M.C., Ascendant, or the Sun's place (if on the M.C. or in good aspect to the Sun at birth) often brings advancement, money gain, and if the transit coincides with a good aspect of Jupiter to the Sun in the Star Courses the good fortune is increased. Jupiter's transit over the Moon's place in the horoscope also brings good luck sometimes.

The transit of Venus over the Sun's place, Ascendant, or M.C. sometimes brings slight benefits; but the power of Venus in transit is very small unless it coincides with a good aspect of Venus to the Sun in the Star Courses.

The transit of Saturn over the M.C., Ascendant, or the Sun or Moon's place, and in opposition to these places, causes ill-health, losses, sometimes a serious illness if Saturn afflicts the Sun and Moon in the horoscope. An adverse transit coinciding with an adverse Star Course of Saturn to the

Sun is of portentous augury and enhances the evil of the Star Course, making the evil more threatening. The worst foreboding may be expected, and even death if the horoscope reveals a weak constitution.

The transits of Neptune and Uranus over the Ascendant, M.C., or the Sun or Moon's place, even when they are adverse Promittors, (*i.e.*, afflicting the Sun at birth) do not bring about such dire misfortunes as Saturn, and they do not appear to seriously assail the health; but they cause loss of money, reverses in business, great disappointments in connection with one's domestic or business affairs.

The transit of the Promittor Mars over the Sun or Moon's place or in opposition thereto when he is retrograde is ominous, for such transits often cause serious bodily hurts, accidents, feverish or inflammatory distempers, strife; but the danger is great indeed if the transit coincides with an adverse Star Course of the Promittor Mars to the Sun. Unless Mars is stationary, retrograde or transiting slowly this Promittor's transits are mostly inoperative.

When Mars and Saturn are in evil aspect at birth subsequent transits in square or opposition to Saturn's position will cause hurts and wounds when Mars is stationary or retrograde.

When Mars and Jupiter are in square or opposition at birth the subsequent transits when stationary or retrograde will cause strife, conflicts, and rash acts.

The transit of Mars (if Mars afflicts ☿ in the horoscope) over Mercury causes quarrels and indiscreet acts; over Venus sudden love-affairs and indiscretions.

The adverse transits of the Promittors Mars, Uranus and Neptune amongst themselves cause conflicts with adversaries, vindictiveness, stress and storm.

The transit of the Promittor Jupiter over Saturn, Uranus or Neptune often brings gifts of money, advancement, gain by will; over the place of Mars when Mars and Jupiter are in good aspect at birth there is much activity, great personal effort and advancement.

When Uranus, Saturn, Neptune and Mars promise good fortune by their good aspects to the Sun in the horoscope then their transits often confer advancement, business and money success and sometimes a good position is obtained.

The adverse transit of the Promittor Saturn over the Moon's place in the horoscope often causes much depression or melancholy. This Promittor's transit over ☿ also causes depression. But the Saturnine depressing influence is most powerfully impressed upon the person when Saturn is stationary and retrograde. A transit of Jupiter over Mercury is likely to bring literary success, if ☿ is in good aspect to Jupiter in the horoscope. Mental effort is stimulated by the transits of Promittors. But they will be misguided efforts if they are evil Promittors.

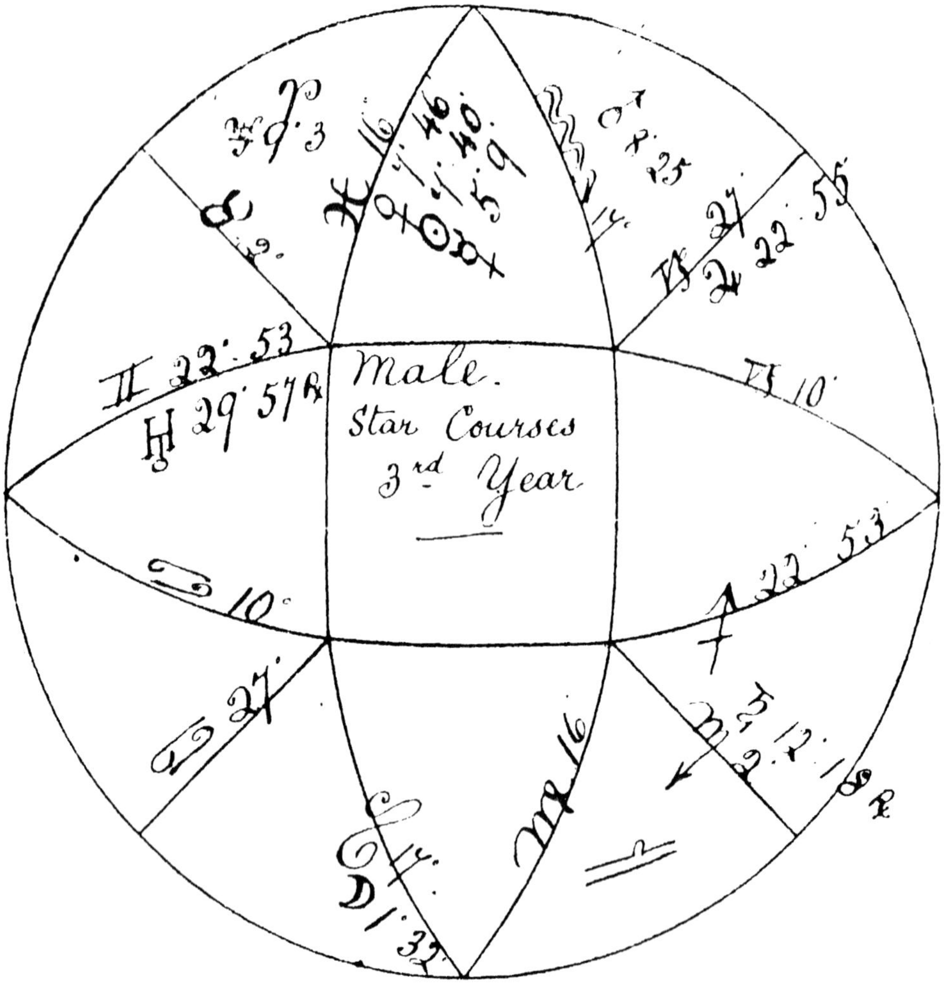
Male.
Star Courses
3rd Year

☉☌♀
☉⊻♆ applying.
☉∠♃
☉⊻♂ applying.
☉∠♃ Radix.
☉⊻♂ Radix separating.

☿☌♀ Radix.
☿☌☉ Radix.
☿△☽ Radix separating.
♀∠♃

The first twenty-four hours after birth represent the first year. Therefore, the third twenty-four hours represent the third year, etc.

1868.
Feb. ☽ 1° ♌ Bq. ☿, sep. Bq. ♀, Bq. ☉
Mar. 2
Apr. 3
May. 4 ☽⊻☽ Radix.
June. 5 ☽ 36° ♅, ☍ ♂ Radix, 36° ♅ Radix
July. 7 ☽ P. ♄
Aug. 8 ☽ ☍ ♂
Sept. 9 ☽ △ ♆, △ ♆ Rad.
Oct. 10 ☽ 162° ♃ 162° ♃ Rad., 36° ☽ Rad.
Nov. 11
Dec. 12 ☽ □ ♄, □ ♄ Rad.
1869.
Jan. 13 ☽ ∠ ♅ app., 162° ☿ Rad., ∠ ♅ Rad. app.

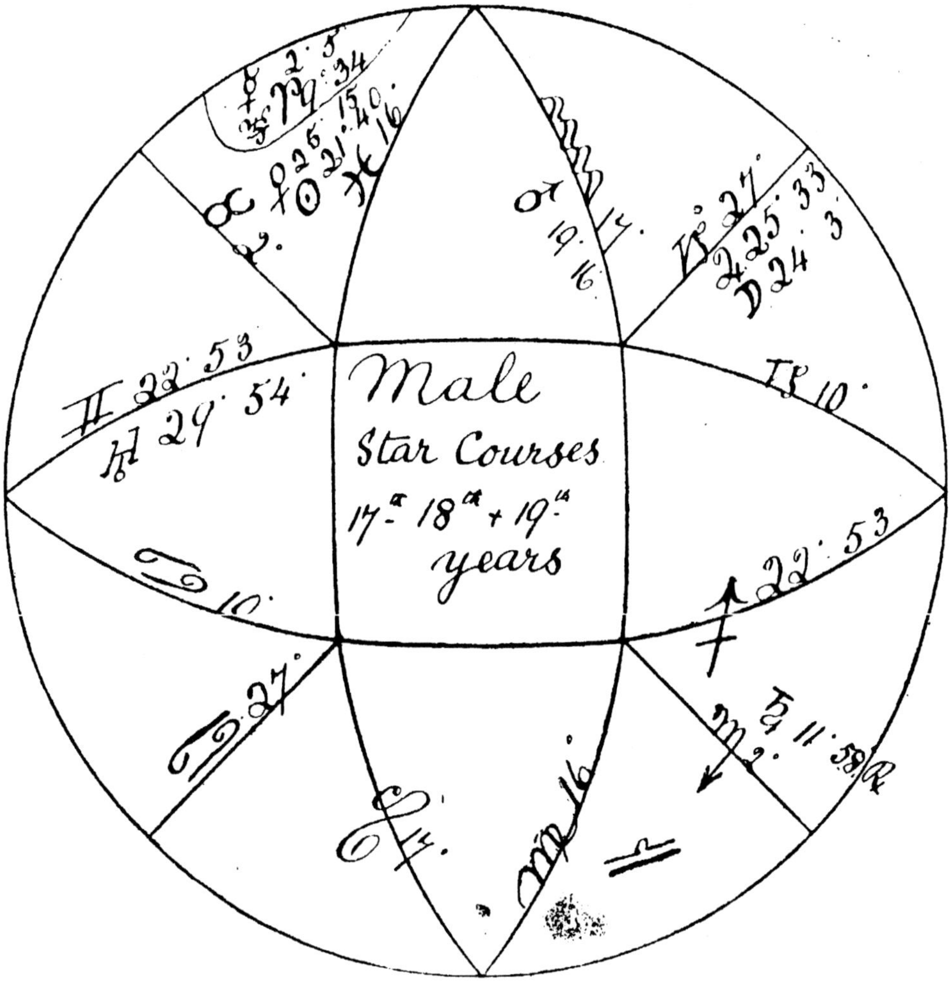

Aspects of Promittors: ☿ semi-sextile ⊙ ☿ semi-sextile ♀.

⊙✶♃ Rad. ♀✶♃
⊙∠♂ Rad. ♀ 36°♂
⊙ 105°☽ Rad. sep. ♂⚼☽ Rad.

⊙22°☿ Rad. ☿∠♂ ♀22°⊙ Rad.
⊙ P. ♆ ☿□☽ Rad. ♀22°♀ Rad.
⊙ P. ☿ ☿ Bq. ♄ Rad.
☿ Bq. ♄
☿ Q. ♃ Rad.
☿⊻♀ Rad.
☿⊻⊙ Rad.
♀⚼♄

1882. *17th year.*

Feb. ☽24°♑ Q. ♄, Q. ♄ Rad., ☌♃ Rad. sep. 162° ☽ Rad. sep.
Mar. 25 ☽ ☌♃, ✶♀, 36°☿ Rad.
Apr. 26
May. 27 ☽22°♂ Q. ♆, Q. ♆ Rad.
June. 28
July. 29 ☽52°⊙, 36°♀ Rad., 36°⊙ Rad.
Aug. 0 ♒
Sept. 1 ☽⊻☿ Rad.
Oct. 2
Nov. 3 ☽✶☿
Dec. 5 ☽52°♀, Bq. ♅, ⊻♀ Rad., ⊻⊙ R., Bq. ♅ R.

1883.

Jan. 6 ☽ ☌♂ Rad.

1883. *18th year.*

Feb. ☽ 7°♒ ☽∠⊙
Mar. 8
Apr. 9 ☽✶ ♆, 22☿ Rad., ✶ ♆ Rad.
May. 10 ☽∠♀, □♄, Bq. ☽ Rad.
June. 12 ☽□♄ Rad., P. ♄
July. 13 ☽52°☿, 22°♀ Rad., 22°⊙ Rad.
Aug. 14 ☽⚼♅, 22°♃ Rad., ⚼♅ Rad.
Sept. 15
Oct. 16
Nov. 17 ☽22°♃, 36°⊙, 52°♆, 52°♆ Rad.
Dec. 18 ☽⚼☽ Rad.

148

☉ □ ♅
☉ 36° ♂ app.
☉ □ ♄ R. sep.
☉ 52° ♂ R. sep.
☉ □ ♅ R.
☉ P. ♀

☿ 52° ♂
☿ Q. ♅
☿ ∠ ☿ R.
☿ Q. ♅
♀ Bq. ♄
♀ ✱ ♂ R.
♀ ⩗ ♀ R.
♀ ⩗ ☉ R.
♀ □ ☽ sep.

Aspects of Promittors:
Sun Semi-quintile ♂.
Venus Semi-sextile Sun.
Sun parallel Venus.
Moon Q. Sun and Septile, early and Spring months.
Moon Sextile Sun, December.

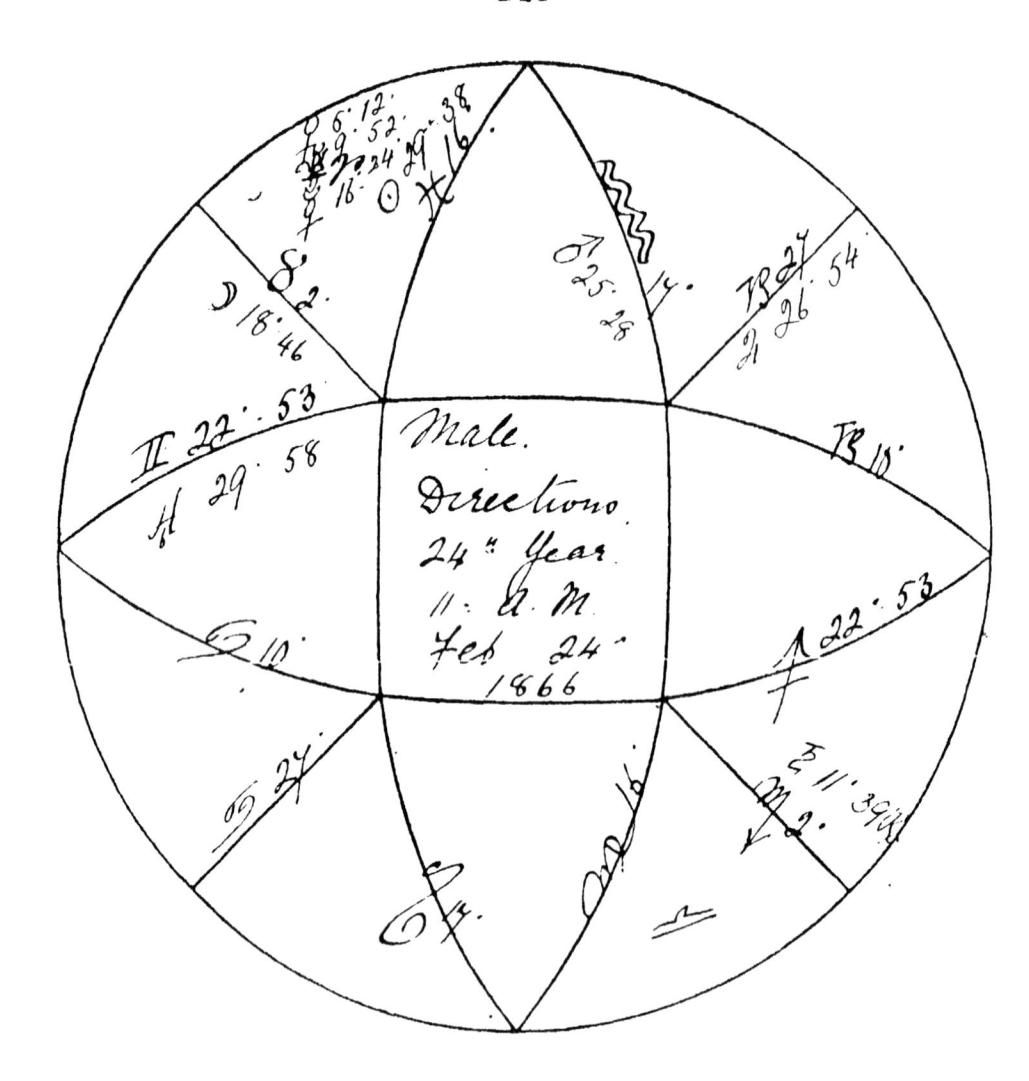

1890.
Feb. 18 ♉ ☽ ⩗ ☿ sep. Q. ♀ R., Q. ☉ R., P. ♂
Mar. 19 ☽ ∠ ☽ Rd.
Apr. 21 ☽ 52° ☉, ∠ ♀, 105° ♂ Rd.
May. 22 ☽ 36° ☿, △ ♃ R.
June. 23 ☽ 36° ♅, 36° ♅ R.
July. 24 ☽ ∠ ♆, ∠ ♆ Rd.

Aug. 25 ☽ □ ♂
Sept. 27 ☽ △ ♃
Oct. 28 ☽ 52° ♀, 36° ☽ R.
Nov. 29 ☽ ⩗ ♅, 162° ♄, ⩗ ♅ R.
Dec. 0 ♊ ☽ ✱ ☉, 162° ♄ R.

1891.
Jan. 1 ☽ 52° ♆, ∠ ♆ app., □ ☿ R., 52° ♆ R.

Star Courses in the 28th year were:—Aspects of Promittors: Sun semi-sextile Mercury. Sun semi-quintile Mars. Venus semi-sextile Sun. In the Spring months of 1893 the Moon was in the 5th degree of the sign Cancer, therefore in trine to Mercury in February and in the Spring in trine to Venus and the Sun's places in the horoscope. These were most powerfully influential aspects for good fortune.

Star Courses in the 30th year were:—Aspects of Promittors: Sun semi-quintile Mars. Sun bi-quintile Saturn. Sun Orb sextile Mars. Sun semi-sextile Venus and Sun semi-quintile Venus.

In the early months the Moon was Bq. Venus and Bq. Sun in the horoscope and in the middle months the Moon was in trine to the Sun's progressive place. It will be seen, therefore, that these were all propitious aspects which would bring Mr. Pearson much success.

The aspects of Non-Promittors were as follows:—The Moon was opposed to Mars in the Autumn of 1895 and was in quartile aspect with Saturn in the first month of 1896, but these aspects we think proved inoperative.

Star Courses in the 34th year were:—Promittors' Aspects: Mercury septile Sun in the Radix Sun semi-quintile Venus. Sun semi-quintile Mercury.

In 1899 and 1900 the Sun was in conjunction with Neptune, but as this was not a Promittor it would not prove very adverse, but it might have caused a little debility, possibly a little trouble with the eyes. But aspects of Non-Promittors are mostly unproductive: they have little power against either the health or fortunes. Mr. Pearson would probably hardly feel this unfavourable influence of Neptune.

The horoscope indicates what you will get and the Star Courses when you will get it. Mr. Pearson's horoscope portrays riches and the Star Courses indicate the years when he will meet with considerable financial success. We have no doubt, therefore, that Mr. Pearson will more than treble whatever wealth he has acquired at the moment of going to press with our second edition in 1909. There are some fine Star Courses from 1907 to 1909 of Promittors—Mercury conjunction Venus, Sun quintile Mars, Sun quintile Uranus, whilst the Moon forms a sextile with the Sun and Venus. The aspect of the Promittor Mars to the Sun is the aspect of physical activity, much energy, advancement; it increases the vitality. The good aspect of the Sun to Uranus invariably coincides with new enterprises. In 1910 there will be good aspects of the Moon to the Sun and Venus which indicate much success. The cross aspect of the Moon to Uranus in the spring months of 1911 will prove rather troublesome; but the good aspect of the Luminaries will make Mr. Pearson extraordinarily successful. In fact, there are the constantly recurring good aspects of the Moon to Mercury, Venus and the Sun; in 1912 these again coincide and will bring much money gain. It seems to us, however, that the cross aspect of the Sun to Jupiter in 1913 will cause too much expenditure or money loss; it may mean litigation, for it will be observed that Jupiter is an adverse Promittor. In 1914 there is again the good aspect of Venus to the Sun and Venus to Mercury, aspects of business expansion, unusual success, they will probably bring honours, new literary ventures. The cross aspect of the Moon to Uranus in 1914 merely means difficulties and annoyances. There are good aspects of the Moon to Mercury and the Sun in 1916 and 1917 which will bring much success. In 1921 the Sun will be in adverse aspect to Jupiter, which will probably cause money loss, too much expenditure and probably litigation. In 1927 and 1928 he has to fear hurts, falls, much trouble from employees. Of course slight accidents are to be feared under the following transits: 1910 Saturn square Mars, 1911 Saturn square Mars, 1916 (Spring) Mars square Saturn, 1917 Saturn opposition Mars, 1918 Saturn opposition Mars, 1920 Mars conjunction Saturn (Spring and August), 1925 Saturn square Mars, 1926 Mars opposition Saturn (closing months), 1932 and 1933 Saturn opposition Mars.

The Star Courses of Mr. Pearson's horoscope prove conclusively that the minor aspects of Promittors to the Sun are more powerfully influential than major aspects of Non-Promittors.

Printed in the United States
47535LVS00002B/59

9 780766 157965